COMMUNITY LIBRARY
3 2301 00266660 4

D1571698

Human Body

A PORTRAIT *of* ANCIENT MEXICO

Human Spirit

9.15.93 – 1.30.94

MICHAEL C. CARLOS MUSEUM
EMORY UNIVERSITY

HUMAN BODY

A PORTRAIT *of* ANCIENT MEXICO

HUMAN SPIRIT

Edited by
CAROLYN E. TATE

with contributions by
BEATRIZ DE LA FUENTE
MARI CARMEN SERRA PUCHE
FELIPE SOLÍS

MICHAEL C. CARLOS MUSEUM
EMORY UNIVERSITY

The catalogue for *Human Body, Human Spirit: A Portrait of Ancient Mexico* has been made possible through a generous grant from

The Coca-Cola Company

The exhibition *Human Body, Human Spirit: A Portrait of Ancient Mexico* has been made possible through the generous support of the Atlanta Committee for the Olympic Games, The Coca-Cola Company, the National Ministry of Foreign Affairs, the National Council for Culture and the Arts in Mexico, and the Consulate General of Mexico in Atlanta.

ACOG wishes to thank its partners and sponsors: The Coca-Cola Company; Eastman Kodak Company; VISA International; Bausch & Lomb; Xerox Corporation; Sports Illustrated; NationsBank; Champion, U.S.A.; The Home Depot; IBM; Anheuser-Busch, Inc.; and John Hancock Mutual Life Insurance Company.

COVER

Young Woman
Gulf Coast
Classic, A.D. 300-900
Ceramic

CREDITS

Translations
LISA DILLMAN
ALEJANDRO RUPERT

Photography
ANTONIA VIZCAINO – GILLES LARRAIN

Design
TIMES 3

ISBN 0-9638169-0-X

Michael C. Carlos Museum
Emory University
571 South Kilgo Street
Atlanta, Georgia 30322

CONTENTS

FOREWORD

The 25th anniversary of the Mexico City Olympic Games is an occasion worthy of great celebration, and a variety of institutions have come together through the present exhibition to honor the traditions and beauty of a part of Mexico's past. As Atlanta counts down the months until its hosting of the 1996 Summer Olympic Games, both countries are at work to establish new common ground in a free trade agreement with Canada, and the entire world looks to this hemisphere to come together as so many other countries find their identities and alignments changing rapidly. The Olympic tradition provides a signal opportunity to underscore how cultural exchanges, like the one celebrated by this exhibition and catalogue, can serve to link people, institutions, corporations, and governments, and to cement bonds between neighbors or between countries separated by vast distances.

Human Body, Human Spirit: A Portrait of Ancient Mexico is both an outgrowth of a desire for cultural exchange and a superb exhibition in its own right. The notion of planning this loan was launched by Dr. Jeffrey N. Babcock, Director of the Cultural Olympiad of the Atlanta Committee for the Olympic Games, in January 1993, and enthusiastically embraced by Consul-General Teodoro Maus, Mexico's emissary to Atlanta. The highest levels of the Mexican government, including Minister Fernando Solana Morales and Ambassador Jorge Alberto Lozoya were swift to see the value of this project, and gave unstintingly of their support, as did Ana Coudurier, Director of International Exhibitions at the Instituto Nacional de Antropologiá e Historia in Mexico City.

Support for the exhibition coalesced as quickly as the planning for the project itself. In addition to the unstinting support of the Atlanta Committee for the Olympic Games, the Consulate of Mexico, the National Ministry of Foreign Affairs, and the National Council for Culture and the Arts in Mexico, we wish to single out the generosity of The Coca-Cola Company, which provided the funds to make this catalogue possible. Atlanta has enjoyed over a century of enlightened support from The Coca-Cola Company, which opens a new chapter of promising relations with the Republic of Mexico through this project.

The undersigned saw their two staffs begin work immediately to bring the exhibition into focus, with the able help of Guest Curator Dr. Carolyn Tate, formerly Associate Curator of Pre-Columbian Art at the Dallas Museum of Art and now Assistant Professor at Texas Tech University. Among those to be singled out for their efforts are Dr. Felipe Solís, Sub-director of the National Museum, Catherine Howett, Elizabeth Hornor, Lori S. Iliff, and Clayton Bass.

The privilege of undertaking this exciting project cannot be overstated, and it is hoped that this is only the first exchange between the Museo Nacional de Antropologia and the Michael C. Carlos Museum. The emerging partnership between Mexico and the United States is appropriately heralded by the loan of some 92 masterworks of Mesoamerican art, which gives dimension and content to the desire of our two museums and two countries to celebrate the Olympic tradition through mutual understanding of the cultural heritage of this hemisphere.

MAXWELL L. ANDERSON
Director
Michael C. Carlos Museum

MARI CARMEN SERRA PUCHE
Director
Museo Nacional de Antropología

PREFACE

In an article on the art of the Olmec, the earliest Mexican civilization to make monuments of stone, Beatriz de la Fuente wrote, "Man is the principal theme of [Olmec] monumental sculpture...I am interested in investigating the particular form in which the anxieties common to the soul of man are expressed in this monumental art." [1] What is true of Olmec art is equally true of the art of the Maya, Aztec, and other ancient Mexican cultures. It is the human figure, not landscape, not abstract designs, not artificial objects in an illusion of space, that forms the core of the Pre-Hispanic art of Mexico. Over and over, these artists expressed in clay, stone, or pigment what it was like to be human in their own time and place.

In the dozen years since this accomplished art historian, Dr. de la Fuente, defined her quest, psychiatrists, historians, and even astronomers have focused on issues of human identity in a cross-cultural perspective. They have shattered notions that a single concept of human identity is universal to all peoples. Instead, they find that a sense of self is developed in relation to and in response to culture. Since 1400 B.C., many unique cultures flourished and declined in Mexico, each influencing the other to some degree but each retaining, often adamantly, its own character. This situation provides a remarkable opportunity to reflect on the diverse ways in which human societies conceive of their bodies, their rulers, their spiritual essences, and of the world beyond but connected to the body: the supernatural.

The body—in contemporary U.S. society, we believe that it is our source of both delight and suffering. Were it not to nourish and comfort our bodies and to enhance a sense of identity, we would not have to work. The head is the seat of our intellect; there, or perhaps in the heart, our emotions reign. Our bodies are a key element in the sexual behavior that mesmerizes us by providing a means of establishing a broader, multi-personal sense of self. Our soul, too, that part of us that remains after the body dies, is somehow attached to the body. Most individuals in our society think that the body forms a tangible boundary for their sense for their sense of self.

Until recently our image of the body has been that of a machine that runs; perhaps, if one believes in a God, sparked by a divine fire or breath. With the contributions of the cultural knowledge of a diversifying American population and with our increasing knowledge of other cultures, however, our concept of the body is expanding. The possibility of controlling the body through the mind and the spirit has been explored in such popular formats as Bill Moyers' television series and recent books, in which people as diverse as Chinese Tai Chi masters and American cancer patients testified to their ability to control bodily energy and physical health through discipline of the mind.

This exhibition examines a Pre-Columbian view of the body as linked, not only to an individual mind and spirit, but also to a community, to a territory where crops flourish and where the ancestors "live," to celestial energies that enter the body and sustain its processes, to an animal spirit companion, to forces of wind, rain, thunder, lightning, earthquake, and fire, and to the conjunction of astronomical and supernatural characters that personify each day.

In certain contemporary indigenous cultures of Mexico and Central America, such as the Mam-speaking Maya, the sense of self does not stop with the body. Members of a community share a community soul in addition to possessing an individual soul. Acting in accordance with tradition strengthens the link to that soul and allows the individual greater access to ritual "heat" or fiery knowledge and power. People define themselves primarily in terms of their community, its lands, ancestors, and traditions. These people also share the reality of dreamtime. Their "dreaming bodies," alternate selves, may meet in dreams where their actions decide the fates of the individuals, only to be acted out while awake. Alternatively, the ancestors may speak to people in dreams, teaching important traditional skills and ritual behavior. Or, people may dream different segments of the same dream, which, when combined, forecast the destiny and activities of the whole community. Clearly the premises that defined the concept of the body, its health, and its relation to other people and to the spiritual world, while foreign to us, served the ancient Mexican civilizations well, forming the basis for a series of intellectually, socially, and artistically complex civilizations of unusual longevity and resilience.

A major intellectual impetus for the selection of the human body and spirit as the theme of this exhibition is the work of Alfredo López Austin.[2] His exegesis of the Nahuatl (the language of the Aztecs) texts referring to the parts of the body, its animating energies and animistic centers, and its relation to the physical and spiritual world demanded that this fascinating topic be pursued using another kind of evidence—visual images instead of words. Using sculpture rather than words as testimonies of past ideas allows us to extend the investigation of the attitude toward the human body to earlier Pre-Hispanic societies which either did not write or who wrote in hieroglyphs or picture writing whose subjects did not explicitly address the kinds of questions we have. The sheer volume of human images in the sculpture of Pre-Hispanic Mexico fortifies a thorough analysis with a seemingly endless source of data. As long as the researcher consistently seeks out indigenous categories of analysis and distinction, rather than forcing the imagery into patterns conceived by the modern Western mind, the message that results should relate strongly to the intent of the artists. These objects were intended to convey, or even possess, spiritual presence. They were made in ritual circumstances for ritual purposes. The spirits of specific supernaturals were installed in many objects during an inauguration ceremony.

While selecting objects for the exhibition from the astounding collection at the National Museum of Anthropology in Mexico City, the curators, Mari Carmen Serra Puche, Felipe Solís, and I brought to bear not only our intellectual forces and aesthetic sensibilities, but also what intuition we could gather in order to assemble a view of the human body and the human spirit that the ancient people might accept. The basic approach was to ask the question, "Which sculptures best express the messages that the ancient people told about themselves?" In their enthusiasm for the project, Dr. Serra Puche and Archaeologist Solís made every effort to secure the finest objects for this exhibition, despite the demands of many other exhibitions traveling abroad from the National Museum of Anthropology this year. It is a great honor for Atlanta and for the Cultural Olympiad to host these important and culturally priceless works of art.

The catalogue essays and the installation create a multi-dimensional portrait of ancient Mexican identity from several vantage points. The three broad themes of the exhibition, each contained in a separate gallery, are "Images of Cultural Ideals," "The Cycle of Life and Death," and "Transformation of Body and Spirit." Each of these topics is addressed in this catalogue by one of the authors, with the addition of a fourth essay which demonstrates the interweaving of subject matter with artistic style.

PROVIDING INSIGHTS to the pieces are the text labels in the galleries and an audio tour. The latter takes the form of a storyteller, allowing indigenous verbal messages to complement the visual ones. Sources of the stories are myths collected in modern times, early Post-Conquest writings by the Aztecs, and a few reports of recent scholarly discoveries.

In the first gallery, we look at the human figure as shaped by cultural values and political demands. Here are pieces from all the major Pre-Hispanic Mexican civilizations, grouped loosely by the roles they portray or the postures they assume. This allows the viewer to compare how culturally imposed artistic canons such as the selection of an activity or stance for the figure, the degree of stylization or naturalism, the selection of a proportional scheme for the figure, the degree of three-dimensionality and modeling in the figure express fundamental attitudes among the individual, the ruler, society, and the cosmos. Looking at the figures of people from across ancient Mexico, we are able to perceive the characters of the cultures who produced the works and to explore visually their varying concepts of political power.

For example, at the entrance to the first gallery, entitled "Images of Cultural Ideals," the magnificent Aztec Standard Bearer of A.D. 1500 *(Plate 1)* is juxtaposed with the Tlatilco Red Woman from 1000 B.C. *(Plate 13)*. In view toward the rear of the room is another Standard Bearer *(Plate 5)*, this one Toltec, and from about A.D. 1100. The Tlatilco standing female figure, her stance serenely symmetrical, with her square face, elongated eyes, continuous brow ridge, and her oval mouth, provides the prototype for the later stone ideal standing males of the Post-Classic period. But there is a pronounced shift of emphasis. The Tlatilco woman is without costume except her headdress, and schematized, with abbreviated arms and a head one third the size of her body, so that the very position of standing symmetrically is the emphasis of the piece. The artist was not concerned with showing a social role for her as much as expressing a state of spiritual or inner balance. While the later sculptures share a similar facial and corporal design, they are rigid, blocky depictions of human beings whose personal interests have been subsumed by the political will.

The catalogue essay, "Political Organization and Artistic Expression in Ancient Mexico," by Felipe Solís provides an enormously helpful chronological framework of political development of Mexican art styles and societies. It describes how the intentions, subjects, and focus of artistic expression changed as societies became more complex.

Dr. de la Fuente's article, "Expression of the Human Figure in Pre-Hispanic Art," examines the formal qualities of the human representations displayed here as related to both the sense of self and the political structure of each society. She traverses the artistic field from the purest schematization or sketch to the portrait, calling attention to specific cultural prototypes that demonstrate the lack of interest on the part of ancient Mexican artist to express personality and a concurrent emphasis on a "depersonalized pattern that shows communion with the community and the rest of nature, of which an individual is an integral part."

In the second gallery, we look at sculptures that illustrate various age and gender roles in the cycle of life and death. In most ancient Mexican societies, the phases of human life were analogous to those of the sun on a daily and annual basis, and to the cycles of plant and animal life. Parents and community members nurtured the growth of children with ceremony and opulent orations. Several such speeches pronounced by the Aztec nobility are presented in the audio tour.

Not often shown in Pre-Hispanic art are groups of individuals involved in the rituals we feel certain occupied much of their life. Perhaps this is because the setting for most of these sculptures was a tomb, which was permanently charged with ritual character by the presence of the figures themselves, by the corpse, and by the prayers that were offered in the burial ceremony. Nevertheless, we still see people portrayed in many phases and roles of life. Certainly gender models were fashioned by ancient artists: for women, the fecund females, the nursing mothers, the elegantly dressed weaving women. Men are generally portrayed as mature or as elders, in the roles of sage, sower, warrior, priest, sacrificial victim, and in some cultures, ruler. An exception is the ado-lescent Aztec sculpture *(Plate 50)*, whose unusual youth the nudity suggest relation to agricultural fertility.

The third gallery shows the human image deformed or transformed by spiritual powers. In Pre-Hispanic Mexico, the process of transformation was perpetual for all things and beings. The model of mutability was the sun, which daily moved from east to west and, as it traveled, changed from white and wan, to hot and yellow, to red and fiery then was consumed by the underworld where it carried on its mirrored existence in the guise of a jaguarian creature, and finally was reborn. Following the pattern of the sun, the physical bodies of humans not only changed during the course of a lifetime, but also regularly as people donned masks and costumes to impersonate deities during rituals, as they interacted with their animal spirit companions, as they shifted stations in the social hierarchy, as they took another form during dreams.

People also deliberately reformed their bodies. The Maya nobility flattened the crania of newborns to elongate their skulls. Many cultures tattooed and scarified their bodies and endured the pain of dental filing and jade inlays. The body was also a medium of sacrifice. In various cultures, incisions were made in the ears, noses, forearms, tongue, or penis to obtain sacrificial blood for the perpetuation of cosmic energy. Those whose bodies were transformed by the gods into such shapes as hunchbacks and dwarfs were considered to be specially favored with supernatural powers. *(Plates 78, 79, 80)*.

Even death was not a terminus but merely another transformation. From spiritual deaths the individual likely revived, living a transformed life. The ballgame is an example of such a battle with the forces of darkness and death *(Plate 72)*. As López Austin pointed out, a person only had to leave the company of others to stumble into a terrain where the supernatural activity was all too intense. A journey in which he had to cross gulches, streams, and forests took him into regions ruled by aggressive beings of horrifying shapes, such as the great woman who died in childbirth, Cihuateteo *(Plate 68)*.

These and other themes involving the human body and the realm of the spirit are discussed in the essay by the present author.

The works of art gathered for this exhibition were chosen to represent as fully as possible the range of human experience in ancient Mexico. This remarkable visual legacy illustrates that, while all these cultures shared beliefs and practices, there simultaneously existed many viable definitions of being human—in both physical and spiritual aspects—and many ways of constructing the reality of the material universe. The task remains for us to recognize the common spark that underlies these wide varieties of human experience.

I AM SINCERELY GRATEFUL to many individuals for the opportunity to serve on this project. I wish to thank Dr. Maxwell L. Anderson and Dr. Rebecca Stone-Miller of the Michael C. Carlos Museum and Dr. Jeffrey Babcock, director of the Cultural Olympiad of the Atlanta Committee for the Olympic Games,for inviting me to fulfill the role of guest curator and for their constant support. It has truly been a great honor and an intellectual delight for me to assist Dr. Mari Carmen Serra Puche and Archaeologist Felipe Solís of the National Museum of Anthropology and their staff in formulating the show and working on the catalogue. From Dr. Beatriz de la Fuente's work I derived much stimulation. I wish to reiterate thanks to the enlightened and enthusiastic leadership and contributions of the Mexican Consul General in Atlanta, Teodoro Maus, of Mexican Minister Fernando Solana Morales, Ambassador Jorge Alberto Lozoya, and Director of International Exhibitions of the National Museum of Anthropologia of Mexico Ana Courdurier. The staffs of both the National Museum of Anthropology and the Michael C. Carlos Museum have been creatively involved in every aspect of the exhibition. Special recognition is due for her skillful management to Assistant Director Catherine Howett, for work on the catalogue and didactics to Coordinator of Educational Programs, Elizabeth Hornor; to the talents of Exhibition Designer Clayton Bass, and to the painstaking care of Registrar Lori S. Iliff, all of the Carlos Museum. Catalogue designer Robert Evans worked with grace and lightning speed to produce this beautiful volume. For her unstinting support of my involvement with this project, I wish to thank Melody Weiler, Chairperson of the Department of Art at Texas Tech University.

CAROLYN E. TATE
Department of Art
Texas Tech University

1. Beatriz de la Fuente, "Toward a Conception of Monumental Olmec Art," in *The Olmec and their Neighbors*, edited Elizabeth P. Benson. Washington D.C.: Dumbarton Oaks, Trustees for Harvard University, 1981, 85-89.

2. Alfredo López Austin, *The Human Body and Ideology: Concepts of the Ancient Nahuas*. Translated by Thelma Ortiz de Montellano and Bernard Ortiz de Montellano. Salt Lake City: University of Utah Press, 1988. Originally published as *Cuerpo Humano e Ideologia: Los Concepciones de los Antiguos Nahuas*. México, D.F.: Universidad Nacional Autónoma de México, 1980.

INTRODUCTION TO THE EXHIBITION

It is an honor for the National Museum of Anthropology to present the exhibition *Human Body, Human Spirit: A Portrait of Ancient Mexico,* which brings together some of the most beautiful and significant representations of the ancient Mexican people.

The National Museum of Anthropology is a point of convergence in Mexico City, where both Mexican citizens and foreigners can admire, in a magnificent place of safekeeping, the principal achievements of indigenous Mexican history.

The contrast of landscapes and sensibilities that form Mexican geography have been subdivided by their natural characteristics into five large regions: the Maya zone, whose tropical forest culminates in a calcareous or chalky plain perforated by sacred natural wells; the area of Oaxaca, with its abrupt elevations of terrain and its mysterious breeze; the Mexican Gulf Coast with its exuberant vegetation, high mountain peaks, and fertile seaboards; in addition to the High Central Plateau, the Basin of Mexico where there are innumerable valleys and lakes, and moderate climate; West Mexico, all mountain ranges and coast; and beyond the limits of Mesoamerica, Northern Mexico with its desert climate and inhospitable regions. The diversity is captured not only in the richness of styles and forms, but also in the raw materials themselves, which range from volcanic rock to precious stones and to the various kinds of clay transformed into subtly textured polychromy. "Mesoamerica" is the term used to designate the areas of Mexico and Central America where the most complex Pre-Hispanic civilizations flourished. Most of Mexico was included in Mesoamerica, but Mesoamerica extended beyond the borders of the contemporary Republic of Mexico.

In order to achieve a better understanding of its development, the cultural area of Mesoamerica has been divided into three great historio-cultural periods, going back to the first millennia before Christ, the earliest of these being the so-called Pre-Classic horizon.

The Pre-Classic or Formative refers to the agricultural village stage, characterized by self-sufficient groups of fishermen and farmers. As agricultural technology starts to advance, societies begin acquiring a greater complexity, and create adminstrative centers that control the economic resources.

Craft specialization can be admired in figurines that are beautifully modeled from clay as well as in finely polished ceramics, which conserve the everyday expression of the people of this period.

The next era, known as the Classic period, pertains to a style of construction that is beautiful and simple, realistic and dreamy, and that under the command of consolidated political groups, created splendorous cities whose vestiges still astonish both those who are already familiar with them as well as those who are not.

Teotihuacan was one of these metropolises, one which achieved over 600 years of splendor. All different kinds of manufactured articles characterize the Teotihuacan artist as a sensitive artist who portrayed with equal skill his gods and himself.

The artists of West Mexico (called the "Shaft Tomb Culture") also demonstrate a surprising degree of specialization in the detailed figures that represent scenes of their daily life always profoundly connected to the environment that surrounded them.

Even during the Pre-Classic period the West Mexican groups were characterized by their fine pottery tradition; however, the beauty and incomparable realism that their ceramics achieved during the Proto-Classic era were unparalleled in Mesoamerica.

The rich region of Oaxaca had two principal periods of occupation: the Zapotec, which during the Classic period seated its capital in Monte Albán, and from which we have brought some deities molded in complicated clay sculptures for this show; and the Mixtec tradition, consolidated in the Post-Classic period, which first appeared as small estates that eventually became one regional state which was to take up the Zapotec legacy once again.

In the center of Veracruz there lived various groups with very particular cultural characteristics; they have bequeathed us with outstanding creations in clay such as the "smiling figures," and also stone sculpture associated with ball games such as the yokes, stone axes, and palm leaf-shaped sculptures coming from the urban center of

Tajín. This variety of local traditions will be called "Classic Central Veracruz Culture" in our catalog.

The impassioned Maya culture is represented by exquisite figurines modeled in clay, in which we can simultaneously observe the cosmetic customs and the daring of these people, as well as admire the exuberance of their ritual paraphernalia.

The Classic period gives way to the Post-Classic, the stage in which the Mesoamerican tradition austerely takes root and renews itself, prevailing throughout the historical development of the period up until the present day.

During the Post-Classic period there is a resettling of the population. A penetration from the north of tribes with different forms of life adds a new dynamism to the formerly established order, bringing, for example, heightened commerce, and wars of the conquest that attain ever-increasing importance.

In the latest phase of this period appears the splendor of the Mexicas, or Aztecs, founders of the famed metropolis México-Tenochtitlan, whose magnificent design so impressed the Spanish conquerors.

The Aztec people, deeply religious, bequeathed us sculptural images of their gods and representations of surely idealized citizens, perhaps as testimony of a pattern of life to be followed not only by the Tenochas, but also by the different ethnicities that made up their multiethnic state.

This show also contains a sample of the archaeology of the groups of the North, situating us in the desert plateaus of northern Mexico; in this region were groups who inhabited the periphery of the cultural area of Mesoamerica, as well as the semi-nomads of the so-called Desert Cultures, and in the convergence of the territory in the southwest of the United States and the northeast portion of our country there flourished the cultures of Oasis America.

The culture of Casas Grandes formed part of this last region of true oases, which contributed to the development of important centers such as Paquime, or Casas Grandes, a town that is characterized by its adjoining houses made of adobe and mud and for finely finished ceramics decorated with geometric motifs, both zoomorphic and anthropomorphic, in red and black on a white background.

This vast geographical and cultural panorama is synthesized by symbolic ambassadors, men and women, who in their stone and clay expression and clothing conserve quite ancient forms of life.

The exhibition *Human Body, Human Spirit: A Portrait of Ancient Mexico* shows at first glance the diversity of the original inhabitants of Mexico, the multi-ethnic face of our indigenous roots and the artistic expression of a variety of perceptions, from several historical moments in the development of Pre-Hispanic societies.

The cycle of life of those peoples is presented in a following chapter as a means for us to approach different ways of living in which birth, death, adolescence, and old age were transcendental for each of the members of the group.

Beyond human nature lies the magic and power of the gods, those mythical beings who in spite of the magnificence of their attributes, were portrayed like men, conceived of with their same attitudes and weaknesses.

All of this ancestral knowledge, and even the physical characteristics belonging to the "men of corn," as they called themselves, the people who were made by supernatural beings, still survive in the ethnic groups who today are distributed throughout the national territory.

This ethnic and cultural heritage is a fundamental element of the identity of the Mexican nation that is currently being transformed and projected according to the changing times in which we live. Our transforming identity creates new possibilities for encounter with other people and other civilizations. As the humans portrayed in this exhibition, who, from remote times and places, were strangers to each other, meet in this exhibition, you will meet them also. More than representing the artistic taste of ancient Mexicans, the exhibition brings with it a part of the experiences and the cosmology of other humans who were the predecessors of the events of our time.

DR. MARI CARMEN SERRA PUCHE
Mexico, D.F., May 1993

PRE-COLUMBIAN CULTURAL REGIONS OF MEXICO

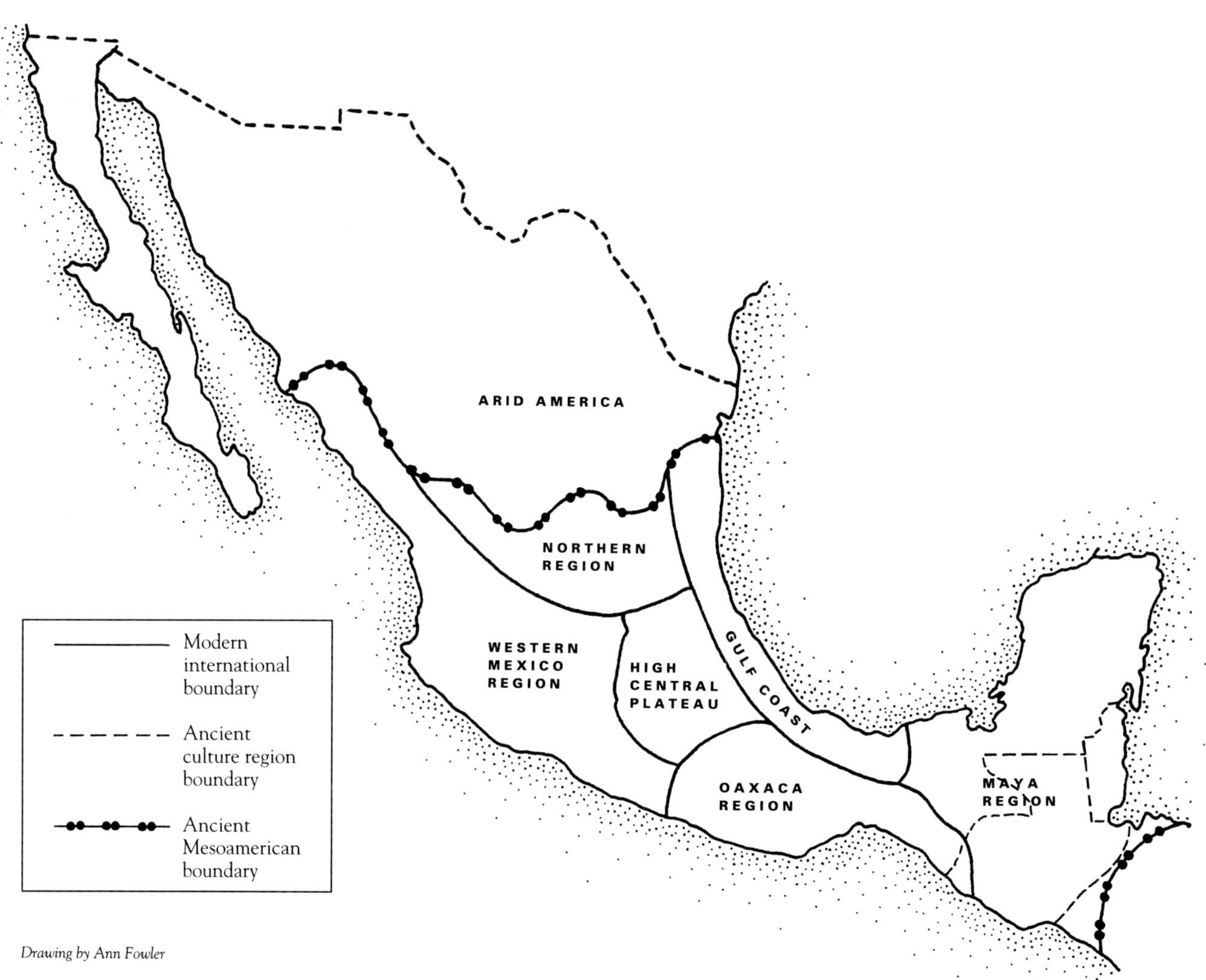

Drawing by Ann Fowler

THE HUMAN BODY AND THE REALM OF SPIRIT

CAROLYN E. TATE

When the Maya Quiche creator gods modeled the present race of humans from ground corn and water, they were pleased with the beings they made, who spoke words of praise, were attentive, walked, and worked. The *Popul Vuh* (the Mayan book of the dawn of life and the glories of gods and men) describes the clarity of knowledge of first humans and its threat to the creators:

"Thoughts came into existence and they gazed; their vision came all at once. Perfectly they saw, perfectly they knew everything under the sky, whenever they looked....As they looked, their knowledge became intense. Their sight passed through trees, through rocks, through lakes, through seas, through mountains, through plains....They understood everything perfectly, they sighted the four sides, the four corners in the sky, on the earth, and this didn't sound good to the builder and the sculptor [the creators]."

The creators decided to diminish the humans' ability to see and blinded them "...as the face of a mirror is breathed upon" (Tedlock 1985: 165-176). The Maya no-longer-seen is what has been called the supernatural or irrational world, and here will be called the unseen or the realm of the spirit. To ancient Mexicans, however, this realm was the omnipresent one entered through dreams and perpetual ritual action.

The sculptures selected for this exhibition were made to be used in ritual, whether part of a household altar, a tomb, or on public view in a ceremonial center. Because of their function, they often embody the beings, activities, and patterns of the spirit realm. Notice that all of them, for example, the Veracruz Female Figure with Red Paint *(Plate 10)* or Aztec Young Man *(Plate 1)*, share an intriguing facial expression. Their gaze never engages the viewer but seems to be focused on some phenomenon that is at once without and within. They seem to perceive, as if in a trance, that which was taken from most humans: the realm of the spirit.

The section of the exhibition treated by this essay, the gallery titled "Transformation of Body and Spirit," explores clues to the ancient Mexican concept of the spiritual world in their portrayals of the human body. The discussion weaves together visual analyses of the objects with written statements by 16th century Indians and observations by ethnographers and art historians that bring the mentality of the ancient Mexican to bear on the themes embodied in the works of art. The resulting patchwork of verbal and visual images represents only a limited view of how spiritual energies transform the human identity and body. As a framework in which to consider the human body and human spirit, the essay begins with a description of the Mesoamerican world view and the human role within it. Ancient Mexican peoples shared ideas quite distinct from ours concerning unseen energies that occupy parts of the body and animate certain qualities or functions of the body. I offer ideas about how these concepts influenced the formal qualities of sculpture, specifically pieces in this exhibition. Bodily deformities and illnesses also engaged the realm of the spirit. Finally, the topic of ritual activity helps complete this brief consideration of the body and spirit in ancient Mexico.

HUMANS AS COSMIC AXIS

Each ancient Mexican civilization, in its conceptual map of the cosmos, expressed its view of its social structure, history, and psychic experiences. Despite regional differences, the ancient Mesoamerican peoples shared profoundly similar notions of a cosmos permeated with forces whose actions affected human destiny in both positive and negative ways. The cosmos was divided into upper and lower realms. The upper, or celestial, realm was generally divided into thirteen levels; the lower realm, or underworld, into nine. Floating on the upper, watery level of the underworld was the surface of the earth and earth's atmosphere, permeated by the forces above and below it. The motions of the wind and rain, the mountains and trees, the caves and waterholes of the earth, and their human-made replicas—pyramids, stelae, tombs, and drainage systems—pierced the levels of the cosmos and acted as conduits for the myriad numinous energies. Both the conduits and the numinous energies were frequently portrayed as monsters or as humans with non-human characteristics, or "deities."

As the conduits were filled with the mutable influences of time, space, the heavenly bodies, ritual acts, and human and supernatural deeds, they changed, constantly transforming shape and character.

Each culture developed spheres of inquiry and action that articulated its sacred cosmic structure. Mesoamerican civilizations shared many such features, including systems for recording genealogies and astronomical and calendric information, agricultural practices timed to the seasons, notions of sacred topography conjoined with cyclic time, social and cultural life dominated by sanctioned ritual activities, emphasis on verbal eloquence and oratory, and the use of art objects to manifest cultural ideals.

Among the high civilizations of ancient Mexico, the body of the ruler was a fulcrum for cosmic forces. One of the unusual qualities of human beings is their predominantly vertical stance, as opposed to the horizontal orientation of most animals. This unique verticality related the human body (and its vascular system), in the Mexican manner of categorizing reality, to trees. Both were conduits between realms, or cosmic axes. Among the ancient and modern Maya and the Aztec, the world tree and humans both reached to the three cosmic levels, roots and feet penetrating to the underworld, trunk and body linking the above with the below, and the branches and arms reaching to the sky. An Aztec document relates the tree and the human body:

[The term *tlac*, "tree trunk"]
has come from people;
it resembles people;
it derives from people;
it proceeds from people;
it is a continuation.

(López Austin 1980: 327 citing Codex Florentino, XI, 113).

The Nahutal terms for the parts of the body also refer to the tree. *Tlac* means the trunk of a tree and the upper part of the human body. The tree's branches are called its hands; the top of the tree is referred to as hair; its bark is its skin; and its wood its flesh (López Austin 1980: 347). Figures of political and spiritual leaders engaged in ritual frequently were portrayed standing in deliberately vertical poses, poised between symbols for celestial and underworld realms. Among the Maya, the principal public image of the king emerges, standing, in relief, from a vertically-situated stone shaft called a *te-tun*, or stone tree (a decipherment made by David Stuart, see Schele 1989: 41).

The concept of the human body as world tree must have been held by the Olmec and embodied in carvings of standing figures in green stone *(Plate 75)*. My studies of Olmec portable sculptures indicate that these small figures of hard stone have been found in Olmec-related Formative Period centers throughout Mesoamerica. The standing figures share many characteristics. The head is always proportionally large for the body. Their limbs are loosely flexed and the knees are bent so that the small of the back is as flat and vertical as possible. In this position, the spine is erect and limbs very relaxed. The mouths are always open and the figures seem to breathe. Many such standing figures were excavated at LaVenta, Tabasco, mostly from tombs beneath the central axis of the ceremonial court. They seem to have been placed near the groin of the deceased, suggesting a relation with his procreative function or with his descendants. Contrary to initial interpretations, (Drucker, et. al. 1959: 152-157), in the well-known group of sixteen standing figures in the National Museum of Mexico, known as Offering 4 of La Venta, no single figure commands the attention of the group. The erect, relaxed, staring figures stand amidst celts, or miniature te-tuns, incised with the images of a flying figure holding a torch and an open-jawed earth monster, together suggesting a passage to the underworld. The Standing Figures, then, are green, in relaxed vertical postures, they appear to breathe, and they were buried upright, all qualities of trees. Offering 4 and the lone Olmec Man in this exhibition seem to depict a group of ritual practitioners concentrating on the vital energies coursing through their bodies as sap runs through the world tree.

THE HEAD, THE HEART, AND THE ANIMATING ENERGIES

Inherent in the human body were centers containing animating entities that produced and maintained life, movement, and psychic functions. These entities originated in the celestial sphere and also in mythical, world-ordering events. In order to instill the animating energies into the individual, rituals were performed at conception, at birth, at the baby's first exposure to fire and sunlight, and at times of special achievement. Since they came from above, animating energies were deposited in the head and from there moved two other principal centers: the heart and the liver. Here, however, I limit the discussion to the head, which, of course, is the center we see, and to the heart.

According to the Aztec conception of the body, the head was synonymous with the sky. The most noble part of the body, it was the head that remembered, that expressed itself, that related to the world, that revealed the person's inner powers. In it resided the animating entity called *tonalli*, a word derived from the Nahuatl verb *tona*, "to make warmth or sun" (López Austin 1988: 204). The *tonalli* involves such related concepts as the warmth of the sun, the day, the "astrological" influence of the day sign upon which a person was conceived and born, and the soul or spirit (Ibid). The *tonalli* provided daily vigor and also promoted growth and development. This belief was not limited to the Aztec, for a Maya Tzotzil term for a similar animating entity, the *k'ul* or *ch'ulel*, still exists today. In ancient hieroglyphic writing, it appears as a small stylized head (God C) that is read *k'ul*, in Yucatec and *ch'ul*, in Chol and means "the spirit," "the pulse," "sacred" and is a quality inherent in certain persons, ritual objects, and cosmic axes (Schele 1989: 36). Rulers, in particular, who in most societies were considered to be descended from divine beings, were potent receptacles for spirit, and had the principal responsibility for maintaining the balance and continuity of the cosmos through ritual actions. The blood that coursed through Mesoamerican rulers was sacrificed periodically as sustenance for the creator gods and ancestors.

In the contemporary Maya Tzotzil town of Chamula, the sun and its motion are the principles that impose order on the physical world as well as humans and their activities. Related to the positive moral value of "up" and the rising sun is the greater importance and symbolic capacity of the head. "Heads and faces of images of saints receive a great amount of attention in ritual action and symbolism, the reason being that the head is the source of heat and power" (Gossen 1974: 35-36).

In many Mexican sculptural traditions, the head and headdress frequently occupy as much as a third of a composition. Consider, for example, the Aztec Young Man *(Plate 1)*, a figure of the ideal masculine form, with a head one-fifth the size of his body, the Olmec Man *(Plate 75)*, the Tlatilco Red Woman *(Plate 13)*, or the Maya Ruler in His Palanquin *(Plate 25)*. The prominence given to the head and headdress in terms of size, decoration, and modeling suggest that the head and the direction "up" carried the same meaning throughout much of Mesoamerica as they do in Chamula today.

Consider also the fact that many Mexican civilizations made images of the head or face alone. Some were made to be worn over the face, some decorated mummy bundles, some were effigies of faces placed on architecture in dedicatory caches. In the Aztec Templo Mayor, the Major Temple in the heart of the capital city Tenochtitlan, face panels made in the distant past (or as replicas of past styles) from the distant regions east and west of Tenochtitlan, were placed in caches that charged the Templo Mayor with the spiritual energy inherent in the face panels. They also formed a potent statement of political and economic dominance over peoples remote in time and space.

The face panels included in this exhibition were not made to be worn as coverings or masks. One, the clay face panel from Teotihuacan *(Plate 85)*, represented an anonymous human presence on an incensario *(Plate 86)*, obscured with symbols such as the mirror. Mirrors were complex symbols in Mexico, representing such things as the sun and fire; the opening to the realm of the spirit, in which one saw oneself; and shining pools of water, another membrane to the Underworld realm of spirit (Miller and Taube 1993: 114-115). The other face panels are abstract images, designed according to the aesthetic of their makers to represent a human identity merged with that of its social group or with the realm of spirit *(Plates 82, 83, 84)*.

COMPOSED ENTIRELY of heads or faces are the ceramic flanged cylinders, probably incensarios, from Palenque *(Plate 73)*. Here we behold the very face of the Sun in the underworld at night. Augmenting the Sun's power and identity are the birds forming his headdress and its chinstrap, perhaps representing another animating energy, the *teyolia*. Lodged in the heart, the *teyolia* could depart the body after death and fly away like a bird. When inside the body, it provided knowledge, emotion and the power of memory.

Hearts are frequently portrayed in art. Well-known examples are those being devoured by supernatural jaguars in the murals of Teotihuacan, those alternating with hands on the necklace of Aztec Coatlique, and in this exhibition, the sacrificed heart superimposed on two crossed pairs of arrows on a relief from Tula, Hidalgo *(Plate 71)*. Perhaps the volutes emanating from the heart on the Tula Relief represent the *teyolia* or a similar animating entity leaving the heart to rejoin and rejuvenate the cosmic forces.

Alfredo López Austin (1988: 60) explains that in Aztec belief, people who exercise spiritual powers, that is, crossing into the invisible world, accepting, rejecting or attracting supernatural influences, manipulating sacred powers, receiving divine fire in the body, and acting through a spirit "double" or entity, the *nagual*, are able to do these things through the energies in their *tonalli*.

In addition to the *tonalli* and the *teyolia*, many Mesoamerican people conceived of another entity that was an integral part of the self. Among the contemporary Maya persists a belief in the *nagual*, ..."a 'spirit double' that shares the life and destiny of its human counterpart," called *kleel* in Maya language Mam (Watanabe 1992: 86). The ability to transform one's animating energies into an animal spirit companion or nagual has been documented throughout Mesoamerica since the 16th century.

The *nagual* generally has the form of an animal. The act of transformation of a human into an animal spirit companion was portrayed in art, especially among the Olmec. The most powerful animal spirit companion, the one most prized by rulers, was the jaguar. In the exhibition is an example of a human-jaguar dual being on the lid of a Post-Classic Maya bowl in the collection of the Carlos Museum. In the collection of the National Museum of Anthropology are such objects as an Olmec stone mask depicting a being part animal and part jaguar, an Olmec human figure in greenstone seated like a feline with a human head, all dating between 1000 and 400 B.C. The concept of human-animal transformation existed among the Classic period Maya as well. On some painted vases, a jaguar is recorded hieroglyphically as the *way* or sleeping spirit of a human (Houston and Stuart 1989).

Independent of the human body but of quintessential importance to its spiritual qualities is fire. Two of the objects in this section are incensarios, or braziers for burning incense in ritual *(Plates 73 and 87)*. Smoky "breath" billowed from the mouth of the Night Sun cylinder from Palenque. This "breath" consisted of burning tree resin, or perhaps strips of paper bloodied in sacrifice. The fire purified these offerings, transforming them into essential heat. People could acquire "heat" through contact with sacred objects such as this and through the repetition of words, song, and actions in the ritual arena. The fire that burned the offerings was analogous to the human ritual heat and to the *tonalli*. Among the Aztec, the act that enabled the gods to give rise to the sun and moon was the blood sacrifice and auto-cremation of a humble and pustulant god, Nanahuatzin, who regenerated from this purifying act of destruction to rise as the sun (Sahagún 1905-1907, fol. 1804).

Even after the gods of Late Post-Classic central Mexican culture had sacrificed themselves to make the sun and moon, there was still no movement in the cosmos. The god of wind, Ehecatl, sacrificed the remaining gods and then blew into the heavens so furiously that the sun began to move. The Ehecatl in this exhibition is a charismatic fat person with a buccal mask, apparently signifying his lips extended while blowing *(Plate 69)*. Like a human, he wears sandals and earplugs. But like a transformational member of the Aztec cosmos, he possesses animal aspects, such as a tail that turns into serpent heads, symbols of another aspect of Ehecatl, Quetzalcoatl. The serpent heads whirl around Ehecatl as if they were his breath, the wind. Ehecatl's breath gave life and movement to the cosmos as breath gives life to humans.

A metaphor of the human body as a receptacle for animating energies is expressed in the hollow tomb sculpture of West Mexico, Oaxaca, Veracruz, and the Pre-Classic societies. These human images were modeled with non-naturalistic proportions and expressively manipulated shapes. Examples of hollow anthropomorphic vessels are the Young Woman from Veracruz *(Plate 49)* and the Colima Seated Hunchback *(Plate 80)*, both sitting in a posture suggestive of meditation.

MARKED BODIES

Certain visible aspects of the human body, especially unusual marks or formations, gave their bearers special powers. In Maya and Aztec civilizations, hunchbacks and dwarves were kept in the royal courts to serve as special messengers who could cross over the barrier to the Underworld. The principal lord or speaker, the *tlatoani*, of Chalco in the Valley of Mexico, sent a hunchback to the court of the rain gods, the Tlaloque, to retrieve an omen regarding the outcome of the war between his kingdom and the Mexica. In order to gain access to the underworld court, the hunchback was confined in a cave in the volcano Popocatepetl and abandoned until he could complete his mission. When the *tlatoani's* servants later found him alive, but starving, he reported that he had indeed visited the court of Tlaloque, and that Chalco would fall, as it did within the year.

The bony Aztec Hunchback recalls this vivid tale *(Plate 79)*. The Colima hunchbacks are also dwarves. The walking hunchback *(Plate 78)* has the stylized wrinkled face of the Teotihuacan Old Man *(Plate 65)* in this exhibition, as well as a bamboo cane and a double headed snake or fish as a vehicle. He leans forward attentively, gazing steadfastly ahead as if listening or looking for a message. The Seated Hunchback sits in a meditative posture as if communicating with the spirit world through his inner energies and their centers *(Plate 80)*.

BODILY ILLNESS AND CURING

The human spirit and an individual's behavior affected the health of the body. One impressive sculpture in the exhibition portrays a woman suffering from large skin eruptions over all parts of her body *(Plate 81)*. She sits uncomfortably, resting on her right side. Little is known about the culture that produced this sculpture, but we might infer some ideas about her experience from colonial Mexican and Maya sources. An Aztec curer (among the Nahua speakers, curers were *ticitl*, a sage, doctor, seer) would undertake several lines of inquiry to arrive at a diagnosis. The physical symptoms were determined, then the seer explored any aberrant behavior by the patient that might cause the ire of the supernatural, sometimes through relation of the twenty day names to the parts of the body as seen in a picture in Codex Vaticanus A. Perhaps divination with sacred stones or beans, which relies upon the ritual calendar for interpretation, revealed the identity of the supernatural attacker. Once the cause was isolated, a cure could be undertaken.

Among the Maya of Yucatan, in whose social order genealogy was critical, the shaman-curer invited the appropriate supernatural beings to attend the curing ceremony, then bound them to the area with ritual actions. With these witnesses, he proceeded to ask the name of the mother and sometimes the father of the disease-inflicting entity in order to exorcise its influence. Its calendric associations and identifying birds, trees, and vines were named. The shaman invoked the spirits of the tools in his medicine bundle to aid him in combatting the offending disease (Roys 1965: passim).

RITUAL: ACCESS TO THE UNSEEN

Being human was a grave burden in Mesoamerica. The creation of the world which people enjoy depended on the self-sacrifice of the gods. The debt for the gift of human life was to assure the continuity and balance of the cosmos. Human actions and words combined in ritual to fulfill this awesome responsibility.

All ritual acts addressed the realm of the spirit, rendering holy the material world in which the acts were performed. An important aspect of ritual was reenacting and thereby teaching mythical events and the ways in which they had repeated over time, including events existing in the memories of living people or documented in writing. Calendar festivals provided for a regular reenactment of such events. Accompanying many rituals were music and dance, frequently portrayed Pre-Classic Highland and West Mexican sculpture, Classic Period Teotihuacan and Maya painting, and Veracruz sculpture. In the exhibition are some figures involved in dancing: the Pre-Classic dancer from the Highlands *(Plate 88)* and the elaborately costumed musicians *(Plates 89, 90, 91, 92)*.

One Aztec warrior-musician has a large bird-like headdress, allowing him to transform identities *(Plate 92)*. When a person wore the costume of mask of a supernatural in Mesoamerica, he merged with the identity of that supernatural, losing some of his own ego in the fulfillment of the primordial act. Among the Aztec, a deity impersonator was a receptacle for the divine fiery energies of the supernatural (López Austin 1988: 376).

The Zapotec *Tlacuache* Priest's human visage (and identity) is almost completely obscured by his huge headdress *(Plate 70)*. According to a Zapotec myth, the *tlacuache*, an animal like an opossum, stole pulque from a rich man and gave it to people to drink. They, however, did not feel good the next day and were weak when the owner of the pulque approached them in anger. While pulque is nourishing and can induce enjoyment, it can also cause drunkenness and improper behavior. Pulque, and the *Tlacuache*, were viewed with ambivalence. As with most powerful forces, their essential characteristics were neither good nor evil but could be used or abused by humans.

In an apparent reversal of roles, an image of a dog from Colima is portrayed wearing a human mask *(Plate 74)*. The fat, hairless dogs (known as *Itzcuintli* in Nahuatl) apparently guided the spirits of their dead masters across the bodies of water in the underworld. We can only speculate about whether this dog wears a human mask to play a trick on the newly dead spirit, or is a vessel for the spirit of the human he impersonates, or the animal soul of a human, or impersonates some deified human in Colima mythology. However, the identity of dog and human are intertwined, and images of beings with animal bodies and human faces form a recurrent theme in Mexican art.

BECAUSE THE BURDEN of perpetuating the movement of the cosmos rested on humans, the human body was a primary source for sacrificial offerings. Sometimes the body itself was modified according to social custom and perhaps also to increase spiritual potency. Many ancient Mexicans filed and inlaid their teeth, enduring what must have been prolonged pain. Note the filed teeth on the large Nayarit Standing Woman and the Zapotec Woman *(Plates 62 and 7)*. Scarification can be seen on several of the images, such as the jaw of the Prisoner from Kum-Pich *(Plate 2)* and the shoulders of the large seated figure holding a bowl from Jalisco *(Plate 17)*. Flattening the cranium was a practice of Maya nobility, visible in the slope of the profile stucco head and on the Polychrome Plate *(Plates 16 and 15)*. Auto-sacrifice of blood is well documented among the Mayas, who bled themselves from their ears, virile members, and tongues. Blood was collected on strips of paper and burned as an offering in the ritual fire.

LIFE AND DEATH were perpetually recycled in ancient Mexico. Recall that the Aztecs (perhaps as a retrospective political manipulation of the creation myth?) explained the origin of the sun and moon by an auto-sacrificial act on the part of Nanahuatzin and other gods. Another example is the regeneration of the ancestors of the great Maya king Pacal of Palenque, who died in A.D. 683. His royal ancestors are portrayed on the sides of his sarcophagus emerging from the earth as young trees. The Aztec rituals involving Xipe Totec, Our Lord the Flayed One, also illustrate the relation between death and life.

The major festival of Xipe Totec fell during the third twenty-day "month" of the year. To inaugurate it, some towns staged gladiatorial combats, then killed the losers and flayed their skins. The victors tied the skins of their victims' faces over their own, then turned the skins of the torsos inside out and wore them for twenty days until they rotted and fell off. At the time of the Conquest, this festival fell during the dry season and thus suggests agricultural renewal, the sloughing of skin by a snake, or of a husk by a seed, allowing a new life to emerge. The Xipe head in this exhibition was the removable top of a large ceramic figure who probably wore a flayed skin *(Plate 77)*.

Every aspect of life involved death. The ballgame was a sport but also a metaphor for the movement of supernatural forces in their aspects as heavenly bodies *(Plate 24)*. The Maya book, *Popol Vuh*, tells of the shamanic death and rebirth of the Hero Twins, prototypes for human behavior, as they battle the Lords of the Underworld. The first twins to descend die, outsmarted by the Lords. The second twins journey into the realm of death to resurrect them, undergoing many trials, including playing ball with the Lords of the Underworld. The second twins undergo several shamanic deaths themselves. Finally reborn in disguise, they defeat the Lords but are unable to resuscitate their fathers, who thereafter are honored as influential ancestors. The second twins then rise as the Sun and Moon or Venus. A shamanic ballgame ritual must have been part of every

Maya ruler's initiation process, for many carried a ballgame title or were depicted on monuments as ballplayers (Tate 1992: 131).

An unambiguous image of death by decapitation in association with the ballgame appears on the Aparicio Tablet *(Plate 72)*. Blood given the form of seven snakes springs from the neck of the headless body. López Austin (1988: 316) noted that among Aztecs, serpents springing from the animistic centers symbolized the escape of the animistic entities' *tonalli* (shadow or double), *teyolia* (spirit), and *ihiyotl* (night air). Here the serpents seem to indicate blood. As mentioned above, among the Maya, blood was the medium of *ch'ulel*, or spirit. Unlike most sacrificial victims, this figure maintained a seated position on a low throne marked by its step-fret support as the entrance to the underworld. The figure is identified as a ballplayer by the yoke, palma, and kneeguard he wears. His right arm crosses his chest in the gesture of submission. If the fate of this glorified decapitated ballplayer was analogous to that of the Hero Twins, he rose from death as a celestial body. This stone is one of a not-quite-identical set from a ballcourt at Aparicio, Veracruz.

For the ancient Mexicans, bodily death was not the end of existence. The parts of the body transformed into various entities. An image in the Codex Laud seems to show the breath of a human turning into an image of Ehecatl: the spine into a skull and the hands and feet into snakes. In fact, it seems that death was just another mode of spiritual transformation. In general, souls of those who died from old age went to live as ancestors in the mountains and continued their agricultural tasks, prayers, and through dreams, their teachings. According to Aztec belief, one's fate after death was determined not by comportment during life but by the manner of death.

The spirit of a woman who died in pregnancy or childbirth was transformed into the inversion of female fertility: a devouring monster who stole children on the crossroads. Cihuateteo, the kneeling death goddess, raised her hands as if to snatch the unwitting *(Plate 68)*. Instead of breasts, open hands appear on her chest. Over her heart is a skull. Her crown of skulls attests to her success in sacrificing children to the underworld. Although most images of this devouring former human come from Tenochtitlan, this one was found in the Aztec town Calixtlahuaca, near modern Toluca.

The final image addressed in this discussion is the Zapotec ceramic half-fleshed and half-skeletal head, broken off a figure *(Plate 76)*. The head has a charmingly delicate pointed chin and a broad forehead. One side has the snub nose and taut visage of a youth while on the other side, the nose is merely a swath of bone and the mouth contorts into a ghoulish grimace. Such images existed in many Mexican civilizations. On one level, they expressed the concept of duality that pervaded ancient Mexican thought. On another, they may have referred to the death and resurrection of a shaman. They also compellingly stated that the essence of existence was transition.

Whether of human or supernatural being, no image in ancient Mexican art or thought can be fit into a single category with finality. Within the dynamic arena of cosmic forces in Mesoamerica, the human body and things both material and unseen were subject to the forces of change, conceived in Aztec thought as movement. Despite, or perhaps because of, the strong value placed on adherence to tradition in Mexican societies, human life was subject to countless forces of uncertainty and change. From birth to death, the body coped with the ineluctable forces of the stars, sun and calendar, of the winds, lightning, and rain, of the demands of family, community, and ruler, of political struggle and threat of capture or sacrifice. One's place in society evolved as one gained in prestige and political and spiritual power or as one transgressed the demands of the gods and society. At night, and in ritual, reality shifted to encompass the realm of dream encounters and journeys to the seat of supernatural forces. The human spirit, that unseen nexus of animating energies pulsing to astronomical and natural rhythms and of bodily centers of perception and emotion, was in constant flux. The spirit and body were enriched through ritual and sacrifice or attacked by malevolent forces. In ancient Mexico, the essence of identity, both bodily, social, and spiritual, was transformation.

1. Sources of information on the human body in Aztec thought have been formulated into a coherent and convincing view of the body and cosmos by Alfredo López Austin (1988) and I draw liberally from his work here.

SOURCES CITED

DRUCKER, PHILIP, ROBERT F. HEIZER and ROBERT J. SQUIER. *Excavations at la Venta, Tabasco, 1955*. Smithsonian Institution Bureau of American Ethnology, Bulletin 170. Washington D.C.: Government Printing Office, 1959.

GOSSEN, GARY. *Chamulas in the World of the Sun: Time and Space in a Maya Oral Tradition*. Prospect Heights, IL: Waveland Press, Inc., 1974.

HOUSTON, STEPHEN and DAVID STUART. "The 'Way' Glyph: Evidence for "Co-essences" among the Classic Maya." In *Research Reports on Ancient Maya Writing*, Number 30. Washington D.C.: Center for Maya Research, 1989 .

HUNT, EVA. *Transformations of the Hummingbird: Cultural Roots of a Zinacantecan Mythical Poem*. Ithaca and London: Cornell University Press, 1977.

LÓPEZ AUSTIN, ALFREDO. *Human Body and Ideology: Concepts of the Ancient Nahuas*. Translated by Thelma Ortiz de Montellano and Bernard Ortiz de Montellano. Salt Lake City: University of Utah Press, 1988.

MILLER, MARY and KARL TAUBE. *The Gods and Symbols of Ancient Mexico and the Maya: An Illustrated Dictionary of Mesoamerican Religion*. New York: Thames and Hudson, 1993.

ROYS, RALPH. *Ritual of the Bacabs*. Norman: University of Oklahoma Press, 1965.

SAHAGÚN, FRAY BERNARDINO DE. Historia general de las Cosas de Nueva España. Ed. by Angel Ma. Garibay K., 4 vols., Mexico, Editorial Porrúa, 1956.

SCHELE, LINDA. *Notebook for the XIIIth Maya Hieroglyphic Writing Workshop at Texas*. Austin: University of Texas Art Deparment, 1989.

TATE, CAROLYN. *Yaxchilan: The Design of a Maya Ceremonial City*. Austin: University of Texas Press, 1992.

TEDLOCK, DENNIS *Popol Vuh: The Definitive Edition of the Mayan Book of the Dawn of Life and the Glories of Gods and Kings*. New York: Simon and Schuster, 1985.

WATANABE, JOHN *Maya Saints and Souls in a Changing World*. Austin: University of Texas Press, 1992.

CYCLE OF LIFE

MARI CARMEN SERRA PUCHE*

Birth, growth, reproduction, and death are the transcendental moments of human existence. In every group and in every culture these moments are celebrated according to the unique conception of the world which surrounds them, and thus they acquire a new character: they become moments of reunion, of renewal of alliances or rivalries, of distribution of wealth, and of communication. In short, they are the times and spaces in which societies establish their permanence.

The Mesoamerican territory was the scene of a great series of transformations in the human way of life from the time of hunting and gathering all the resources necessary for survival to the time of construction of the great cities based on tribute; from the time of wandering in search of new places in which to live until humans learned to take possession of their surroundings. All of these transformations are reflected in the use people make of their spaces and take form in the representations of society, the elements of the environment, and themselves.

Mesoamerican society was basically uniform in most of its aspects: economic, religious, social, and political. However, within such a large area which included so many and such different geographical zones, we find many varied customs and traits.

Among the Pre-Hispanic population, according to what can be inferred from the study of graves, life expectancy was short. Although it increased as the societies became more complex, there exists data indicating a great index of mortality between twenty-one and thirty-five years of age with a small population of mature adults and even smaller of older adults, meaning older than fifty-five.

With help from the written historical texts of the European chroniclers during the early years of the Spanish colony, by means of the archaeological remains that have survived to our day, and through knowledge of today's indigenous groups, we are able to come closer to the ways of thinking with which the Pre-Columbian peoples ordered and made sense of the different moments of life.

MARRIAGE AND FAMILY STRUCTURE

A man and a woman, as portrayed in figurines and sometimes in manuscripts, that exchange a tender look, that hold each other's hands and furtively embrace, permit the scholar to imagine the amorous feelings of the people of the past which are rarely portrayed in the archaeological evidence *(Plate 35)*. Besides, representations of this type of scene are scarce in Pre-Hispanic Mexico, and the existing information from the sixteenth-century texts refers in a more specific way to what sexual norms were accepted and were not accepted by society.

Among the Aztec, the most fully documented Mesoamerican culture, marriage involved the union of the *tonalli* or the spiritual entity of each contracting party. The "breath of life" of the two individuals was joined near a large bonfire during the wedding ceremony, thus uniting their lives forever. This conception idealized marriage, an institution which brought stability to a society looking to reproduce itself but always under the conditions that public order dictated.

Among the Maya, a great wedding celebration was organized in which a priest, chief, or elder tied the robes of the contracting parties and carried out a ritual in which he urged the couple to live a virtuous life; afterwards a large party was held in which the relatives of both participated.

Marriage was a bond which could be broken, but to make that decision was difficult since there was moral disapproval by society at large; however, it could proceed in the case of abandonment, sterility, or for failing to perform fatherly duties.

The nobility had the privilege of polygamy as did some warriors distinguished in battle, although formal marriage was limited to one principal woman. In contrast, adultery among the common people was punished with severity after a public trial that could end even in death.

**With Karina R. Durand V. and Manuel de al Torre*

PREGNANCY AND BIRTH

Among some figurines of women from the early and middle Pre-Classic period of the High Central Plateau, it is possible to clearly distinguish the second and third trimester of pregnancy *(Plates 38, 39,40, 41)*.

We know that the process of pregnancy was highly ritualized in the years preceding the conquest as well as among the differing communities of Mesoamerica. From the moment the woman knew herself to be pregnant, ceremonies were held in which advice was given and a chaperone selected who would accompany the pregnant woman and make sure that she did not strain herself and that she ate properly.

It is known that in some groups of the Gulf of Mexico coastal region, the father was also an object of concern and he even had to rest during his wife's labor.

In Pre-Hispanic societies, death during childbirth was common and thus was compared to—at least in those groups to which the written texts refer—the moment of agony. Among the Aztecs, the pain of childbirth was likened to the struggle in battle; in a society in which the work and blood of every individual were precious goods, it was as heroic to give birth to a new member of the group as it was to capture a prisoner in war.

The value of the woman in childbirth and the welcome given to the newborn were reiterated during the moment of birth which was assisted by the midwives.

BIRTH RITUALS

The role of the midwife during birth was at the same time both therapeutic and ritualistic. She bathed the woman in labor and would offer her an herbal beverage to help relax the muscles so as to facilitate the child's birth; she would deliver the baby and wrap it, all the while lecturing the infant on his future earthly life. Later, she would cut the umbilical cord and bury it under the hearth if the newborn were female and, if the baby were male, she would leave the cord to dry and later take it to be buried in the battlefield. The elders of the family were in charge of calling for a calendar diviner, or seer, so that he could name the child and predict his or her fate according to the day and time of birth.

A cultural trait characteristic of Mesoamerica was the intentional deformation of the head. These practices conformed to certain patterns of physical embellishment but perhaps they also had a ritualistic purpose or were to signal a certain social rank. The deformation was achieved by the use of bandages and tablets which were pressed against the baby's skull. The earliest depictions of this custom are found among agricultural village cultures in which it was common to use cradles to deform the skull, that is to say, small beds, in which the child was held while his head was pressed. In this exhibition are examples in ceramic of this practice from the Western Mexico village of Chupícuaro *(Plates 44, 45, 46)*.

Many years later the youth would be submitted to other deforming practices and mutilations in order to augment his beauty: the filing and perforation of the teeth which were sometimes encrusted with precious stones; or the perforation of the ear lobe, the nasal wall or the lower lip in order to place in them adornments of varying quality made of clay (the simplest), obsidian, rock crystals, or precious metals.

INFANCY AND EDUCATION IN THE HOME

In historical sources can be found descriptions of the Aztec family and how from an early age, between three and four years, the children were educated in the rules of politeness that included both service and assistance to their parents in economic activities.

Particularly among the Aztecs, a child's work was considered a part of a broader and stricter education which included ways of dressing and talking, signs of respect towards other members of the group, and in general, work was extolled as a way of "avoiding vices that idleness tends to cause." With that end, it wasn't unusual for correctional measures to reach the extreme of making children bleed with maguey needles or of leaving them tied up all night outdoors.

In other areas of the Mexican territory and in eras prior to the Aztec period, the relationship between adults and children must have been more relaxed. Not so infrequently, there have been found small sculptures which show children in the arms of their mother or small family groups in which affectionate parents share their activities with the children *(Plates 47, 48)*. Such figurines originate from every corner of Mesoamerica and belong to eras dating back to the time of Christ.

ADOLESCENCE AND INSTITUTIONAL EDUCATION

The rites of adolescence have as their goal the integration of the youth into completely productive groups. In different cultures they share a symbolism which has as its objective to mark the end of infancy and the initiation of a new social status.

It doesn't appear that puberty was especially celebrated among the Aztecs except for the entrance of the adolescents into the *calmecac* or *telpochcalli* schools discussed below. The Mayas, on the other hand, held a big party which is still celebrated to this day.

In the Aztec era every adolescent was obliged to attend an educational center. There were various types of schools in the cities and towns of this era: schools for males, *telpochcalli* in each neighborhood and city and a more important school in a sacred precinct where the art of war was taught; schools for girls, *ichpochcalli;* co-ed schools, *cuicacalli*, where dance, song, poetry, and oratory skills were studied; and the *calmecac* schools in which the science of government, traditions, and art were taught to the children of the rulers and renowned traders.

In the Maya celebration of adolescence, the youths,

both male and female, would leave behind their childhood names and adopt that of their parents. They would go to the ceremony accompanied by an older adult of the same sex. The rituals, which consisted of diverse purification rites and the investiture of insignia from the adult world, were directed by the community elders.

In the Aztec world, the beginning of adulthood was marked by the end of the schooling stage which preceded marriage.

THE ADULTS AND THEIR SOCIAL ROLE

The rights and responsibilities of the individuals in the life of the group varied according to their age and social position which was reflected in all aspects of their lives. The nobility of the highest rank, besides all their privileges such as land ownership, could receive tributes and occupy important positions. They were the only ones who could eat venison and wear cotton clothing.

The common people were the agricultural laborers, warriors, and artisans of the lowest rank. They were obliged to work the fields and pay the tributes; rarely did they eat meat of any kind and their clothing was made from agave, or century plant, fibers.

However, this hierarchy was not permanently fixed: a warrior who distinguished himself in battle was awarded a large compensation and a talented youth could be chosen to become a future priest.

In Aztec society, the ideal or prototype of the woman was one who dressed with simplicity and cleanliness, that spoke with clarity and harmony, that walked with composure and did not raise her head too high. She needed to win the admiration of all by knowing how to manage her house with both sense and firmness. She ought be an industrious woman who also prayed several times each day.

For his part, the male was admired for his obedience and reverence. He needed to be attentive to the words of his elders and do whatever they ordered with both diligence and discretion. However, he also needed to be brave in battle where he should demonstrate a strong heart and great spirit; to conquer and to capture prisoners, and even to demonstrate anger in the attack.

The variety of positions and occupations in Pre-Hispanic Mexico was determined by the complexity of each socioeconomic group then found in national territory. It is reported that as early as the Formative era there existed specialized shops in the production of ceramics, stonework, and basketry, all of which survived until the formation of the militaristic states.

In the first cities, specialists in construction certainly existed, as did expert craftsmen in stucco and mural painting, in artifacts made with precious stones, and in trade and in many other areas. By the same token, the growing complexity of society implied the appearance of specialists in social control through civic, religious, or military positions that, at the same time required an extensive bureaucracy to complete their mission.

Later on, those professions multiplied and became even more specialized when the military states increased their dominions well beyond their capital cities.

In this way, we are able to find in the archaeological evidence of Pre-Hispanic Mexico, as shown in great detail in this exhibition, women zealously grinding corn *(Plate 59)*, worried about the preparation of food, or women in the process of creating textiles with which to make the family's clothes *(Plate 60)*. We can also see men of every age confronting the chores of the fields and mothers who, between their arms shelter their little ones. In summary, it is this great variety of occupation which demonstrates the level of development of the Mesoamerican cultures: we see men and women working with precious stones and involved in ceramic production and feather work; we also see traders and porters, priests, seers, fishers and hunters, musicians and dancers, curers or shamans, scribes, lords, warriors, and an interminable list of other professions.

THE ELDERS

Up until the end of their lives, people did not stop carrying out their labors in home and community; it is in this manner that the elders played an extremely important role in society and occupied a privileged spot among the Mesoamerican peoples. The elders were experience; they were the source of knowledge, the example of virtue and in general, of a dignified life.

Inside the family, the older members had the responsibility of guiding the fates of the younger members along the path that society indicated. In the community, elders acted as counselors and judges of public life and their opinions carried great weight on the decisions of the functionaries during the celebration of rituals. Among the pieces that make up *A Portrait of Ancient Mexico*, are found some of these elders, made from clay, which have survived to this day, showing us their experience in the soft wrinkles incised into their faces *(Plates 64, 65, 78)*.

SICKNESS

Both the study of skeletal remains and the study of figurines provide precise information about physical characteristics, sickness, and some demographic data about Pre-Hispanic populations. In general, the investigators have detected from the study of skeletal remains of agricultural populations, the presence of diseases such as rheumatism, arthritis, and some ailments such as parasitosis and nutritional deficiencies.

When social development was complicated by the establishment of the first states' formations, agricultural development and the domestication of animals became sparks for the infection of ailments that until that time had been unknown to these groups.

Population growth complicated even more the

transmission of diseases that were spread by a lack of disinfectants and the contamination of sources of water.

Among the archaeological materials of most interest in the study of sicknesses in the Pre-Hispanic era are the human figurines made during the Classic period in Western Mexico *(Plate 81)*. The sculptors of Mexico stand out for their detailed and careful representation of the human body which acquires in these works attitudes and expressions that are both naturalistic and of a great artistic sensitivity.

In these representations, a series of infectious and deforming diseases have been identified in detail. These diseases, which pained the Pre-Hispanic population, were combatted with a tradition rich in the use of plants and medicinal herbs, a practice which is still alive and which has enriched today's pharmacopeia. There is also surprising evidence of surgery—trepanation in the Oaxaca area—and traumatology or emergency care for the treatment of various physical problems.

On the other hand, some diseases were thought to be caused by curses, evil spirits, or a violation of taboos. Their treatment corresponded as such, to those who possessed the powers to treat such elements: priests and sorcerers.

THE DEATH RITUALS

Pre-Hispanic tradition placed death not as the end but rather as a form of extension of terrestrial life. In tight relation with the death rituals themselves, we find the actual conception of death and the possible transcendence of humanity beyond its physical limits.

We know that in the Aztec period, one's fate depended principally on one's form of death: if the cause of death was related to water, a paradise presided by the rain deity awaited the deceased with flowers and song. The warriors killed in battle and the women who died in childbirth shared the honor of accompanying the sun in certain years on its daily rise. At the same time, the treatment given to the bodies depended on the fate that awaited that particular individual.

The majority of bodies were buried in simple graves underneath houses or sometimes more elaborate tombs. Archaeologists have found different types of burials: some infants were found deposited in ceramic urns; some adults were shrouded with straw mats and covered with red pigments; other bodies were accompanied by rich offerings and objects of daily use; men and women were sacrificed during the construction of an important building; and curiously, some bodies have been found to have animal companions destined to guide them in their travels through the world of the dead *(Plate 74)*.

In ancient Mexico, there were few monumental constructions with funerary purposes. One tomb discovered thus far in the Maya area consists of a death chamber and a pyramid with a temple atop it. The construction of tombs was common in Oaxaca by the Zapotecs, contemporaries of Teotihuacan civilization. The Zapotecs developed a clearly funereal architecture. At the same time, the examples of shaft-tombs of West Mexico are interesting because they imply the development of a complex technique for the creation of subterranean spaces in which the bodies were placed with many rich and elegant offerings. These have provided valuable information about these past societies.

Some cultures of Pre-Hispanic Mexico were accustomed to human sacrifice and cannibalism with ritualistic characteristics. These practices formed a part of and can be explained through a vision of the cosmos which saw sacrifice as a way of communicating with the gods and of fortifying the world.

IN THE CYCLE OF LIFE, the ancient Mexicans brought together cultural patterns which were developed and transmitted from generation to generation. Currently a part of those uses and ancestral customs survive and strengthen a nation in which the family and the significant moments of mankind's life still constitute an important factor in society's cohesion.

BIBLIOGRAPHY

DAHLGREN JORDÁN, BARBRO. *Una vida indígena*. El esplendor del México antiguo: 689–278. Series for the Center for Anthropological Research of Mexico. 7th edition. México: Editorial del valle de México, 1988.

DÍAZ DEL CASTILLO, BERNAL. *Historia verdadera de la conquista de Nueva España*. Biblioteca Porrúa edition. México: Editorial Porrúa, 1955.

LUCENA SALMORAL, MANUEL. *América 1492: retrato de un continente hace quinientos años*. Milán: Anaya Editoriale s.r.l. 1990.

QUEZADA, NOEMÍ. *Amor y magia amorosa entre los aztecas*. For the Center for Anthropological Research of Mexico. México: Universidad Nacional Autónoma de México, 1984.

SAHAGÚN, FRAY BERNARDINO DE. *Historia verdadera de las cosas de Nueva España*. Biblioteca Porrúa edition. México: Editorial Porrúa, 1956.

EXPRESSION OF THE HUMAN FIGURE IN PRE-HISPANIC ART

BEATRIZ DE LA FUENTE

Representing human form is both a necessity and a fundamental problem in the development of consciousness. Only this fact explains the extensive variety of anthropomorphic representations throughout the course of history. The human figure is an image that has been made, unmade, and remade ever since man established systems of visual communication. Hence its essence: the reproduction of man in constant transformation. The visual image is constructed according to the knowledge and beliefs that are gestated and crystalized in a particular society at a determined time, in a manner that reveals the changing conditions of cultures in different periods, and in different directions.

In the historical process, humans have maintained different relationships with nature. I am going to refer, briefly, to those that I consider fundamental and that are revealed in their representations of human figures.

The integration of people and nature defines certain historical and cultural times. Humans have been an integral part of nature, have lived together with it, and shared nature with the other creatures who dwell in its midst; hence people represent their image with both animal and plant features, all of which are the essence of earthly life. Nothing in these images physically or spiritually individualizes any person. Just one image is sufficient to call forth the memory of the whole genus, of the community. The same thing occurs with an image of a jaguar or a serpent; it evokes all jaguars, all serpents. Similarly, when a human figure is portrayed, it recalls all those of its species; all of the attributes that identify humanity become present in a single image.

And yet this symbiotic interaction between humanity and nature leads people to picture themselves as a sketch, emphasizing only those elements they wish to communicate: sex, condition, hierarchy, activity.

When a person begins questioning himself about his own existence, and that of other living creatures, and aspires to comprehend the order of the universe, he initiates the process of separation from nature. This is when a person attempts to transform his appearance in imitation of the gods who grant good fortune or cause calamity. And accordingly, at this point the images of fantastic beings who maintain a human body structure are added to the anthrozoomorphic images.

With the domination of the land and the stability of life in society, humans accentuate their distance from nature. Now they control it, they make it their primordial sustenance, they develop a system of rites and beliefs with which to confront it. Humans also learn to register their feats in this world, depicting their own personality, reproducing victories, and entering fully the path of history.

Various modes of linking oneself to nature can be observed in the representations of the human form from the Pre-Hispanic world. On the basis of this, I will approximate that which is communicated by the faces and bodies, both clay and stone, that are seen in this exhibition. They form a sufficiently significant sample that approach some of the most outstanding artistic expressions of ancient Mexico.

I should point out that the forms of expression themselves are not evolutionary. Human beings, quite simply, know themselves and know the natural world surrounding them according to a very specific relationship to nature. For that reason, the situations relative to humanity and nature are unstable and changing. One cannot, and perhaps must not, imprison the expression of the human figure in rigid standards created by the eager desire to understand the Pre-Hispanic past.

THE NATURAL IMAGE: FROM SKETCH TO PORTRAIT

Although the human figure is always recognizable as such, there are nevertheless different ways of representing it. These range from the purest schematization and synthesis in the general appearance and facial characteristics, to the most astonishing similitude and realistic physiognomy.

Indeed, on the one extreme are those shapes inscribed in geometric patterns: rectangles, squares, and angles if they are flat; rectangular and triangular prisms, and cubes if they contain volume. The features that can be detected in the face, body, and extremities of these figures are minimal; their visual category fits into a schematic type.

On the other extreme are the portraits: those which, without a doubt, attempt to reproduce the physical characteristics, the looks, the gestures, the postures, and the expression of an individual with the greatest fidelity possible.

Between the two extremes, in a sort of intermediate situation, there is room for stylistic variations—a Teotihuacan figurine does not resemble a West Mexican figurine. All have as common ground the fact that they do not excessively deviate from the natural model; they maintain constant features and do not attempt to accentuate any individualizing elements. This category is the most frequently seen in the world of Pre-Hispanic plastic arts, and its works are the most representative of the various styles.

THE SKETCH

Reduction to the absolutely elemental is the characteristic that unifies and groups together figures in this visual category. There is an almost complete lack of detail, except when it is to indicate gender or to show some sign of hierarchy. There is a desire to transform the human body into outline form, to make it static, sometimes rigidly inalterable—sculptural movement is constrained to contrasts of plane or volume. There are no bodily or facial expressions, nor are there gestures. Sometimes, due to their simplicity, the features resemble caricatures.

This is where the Aztec-Mezcala style masks and the anthropomorphic pots from Casas Grandes come into play *(Plates 82, 85, 11, 12)*. Here it is fitting to explain that although it is true that the objects can be grouped together by the visual elements that they have in common, this procedure is just one methodology for their study and comprehension, since in reality each piece has its own sculptural individuality. With this in mind, it is now of interest to highlight the common factors that legitimately allow the works to be grouped together. The objective is to demonstrate the most notable expressions of diversity.

One of these masks is a simple diagram, quite abstract from visual reality *(Plate 85)*. Planes and slight projections make up the features. Inscribed in a trapezoid with a small base, the features are organized in successive horizontal rows; thus the forehead, as is common in this sort of face, is a raised flat strip that extends horizontally; the eyes are two horizontal grooves; the mouth is likewise another horizontal channel. Precisely in the center of the face, the nose projects itself like a vertical strip that divides the face into two symmetrical parts. This simple composition, perfectly harmonized, shows that which is immutable, that which does not change; hence its inexpressive quality.

In fine-grain stone, polished to the extent that it reflects like a mirror, the other mask exhibited here has, within the pattern already described, aspects that characterize it *(Plate 82)*. The lines curve, creating subtle concave and convex sets, formally shaping the facial features. The silhouette in which this mask is inscribed is an oval cut in the upper part, at the height of the forehead; the ocular cavities are ovals beginning at the base of the nose and extending broadly all the way to the temples; the mouth is, in turn, an oval cavity; and the prominent nose is characterized by rounded nostrils. Its static expression is animated by the reflection of the stone and by the combination of lines and curves from which it is formed.

Also schematic are the anthropomorphic figures found in the vases of Casas Grandes *(Plates 11 and 12)*. However, their essential simplicity responds to a different vision. On one hand, the formal intention favors rounded forms that are expressed in a pleasing fashion simply due to the roundness of the vessel in which they are integrated; on the other hand, there is also an emphasis placed on demonstrating the gender of the subjects. They are plump figures, seated with their hands placed over swollen bellies or inflated legs; it is worth noting the lack of interest placed in trying to represent harmonious relations of the visual details: the legs are disproportionately voluminous and the arms appear to be long, narrow strips which have been superimposed; the chubby-cheeked faces have round, wide eyes; the mouth is a minimal groove; the narrow lopsided nose reinforces the fact that the appearance has little to do with realistic facial features. It is fitting to add a last consideration: the geometric designs with which the head, face, body, and extremities are adorned. In this way, the simplistic reference to visual reality causes the figures to lack any liveliness of expression; their charm, rather, derives from the apparently naive combination of round shapes and geometric designs. Masks of the Aztec-Mezcala style, anthropomorphic vases of Casas Grandes—two modes of stylizing reality, two formal solutions in which the human, in its universal genre, is reduced to its most elemental expression.

THE CONVENTIONAL MODEL

In the wide variety of human figures whose features do not stray from the natural model, there are many in which the objective is not to represent individuality, but rather the generality of real physiognomy. Nothing is distorted nor particularly schematized. Neither are features replaced; as a whole such human images do not differ substantially from the living model, but rather they are sorts of reiterated tendencies in which a shared conception of the world is underscored.

This way of representing the relationship with nature is due, principally, to the fact that the image, repeated tirelessly, fulfills its purpose. Not perceived in this form of representation is the human drive to find the self in its various dimensions; what is interesting is the exhibition of a depersonalized pattern that shows communion with the community and with the rest of nature, of which an individual is an integral part. This explains the shape of the prototype imposed by the conventional styles of representation.

The individual does not count fundamentally as a person, but is subject to religious, political, and social control. His various aspects are subordinated to diverse cultural values.

Conventional images of men, women, and children dominate the sculptural arts of the Pre-Classic period, of West Mexico, of Teotihuacan, the Toltec and Mayan-Toltec, the Huastec, and in not a few cases, the Aztec. This is clearly illustrated by the objects presented in this exhibition.

AMONG THE MOST ANCIENT representations from Mesoamerica are the figures of women. They are small terra cotta sculptures, between 15 and 30 centimeters high, that in the earliest times were crude representations of feminine forms. *(Plates 30, 31, 32, 33, 38, 39, 40, 41)* Towards the middle of the Pre-Classic period (1150-550 B.C.) they came to have exquisite forms and extraordinary manufacturing. There are two more frequently represented types: young women with narrow waists, wide hips, exceedingly short arms, and stylized legs ending in very short and very pointed feet; and older women who either have pregnant stomachs or else, in an expression of maternity, hold children in their long arms. At first known as "pretty ladies", they magnificently exhibit their naked sex and, although the hands that craft them create them differently from one another, they all share the freshness of the early beauty of woman, in which the characteristics perceived as particularly attractive are accentuated: small, firm breasts, very narrow waists, prominent hips, delicate facial features, hair that falls sensually over the shoulders. These images communicate the endless beauty of the young woman and of the potentials of her fertility, and, above all, of the eternal feminine charm that, under various cultural circumstances, creates a restlessness always present in human universality.

The primordial message of the other group of Pre-Classic feminine figures is the potential of the always fertile woman. These women, mature in appearance, with pregnant bellies and flaccid breasts, repeat the same conventional facial characteristics as the aforementioned "pretty ladies": elliptical and extended eyes, short noses that join up with the eyebrows, small mouths and abbreviated curved chins. It is worth pointing out one significant difference in the expression of their condition: while the young women are standing, the pregnant ones are seated. This posture reinforces the eloquence of their form.

In western Mexico, where today lie the states of Michoacán, Colima, Jalisco and Nayarit, once lived peoples who are known, among other things, for the fabrication of hollow terra cotta sculptures that represent men, women, children, plants and animals. Their destiny was to accompany the dead in their graves. These objects, expressing a love of life, commemorate daily existence although they remain confined in dark necropolises. Although human figures predominate, the abundant presence of plants and animals already indicates the desire for integration with the natural world.

Regional and temporal styles can definitely be noticed in West Mexican (also called Shaft Tomb Culture) funerary art. A common theme in the human-shaped figures unifies them: they are fundamentally beings at work in their daily activities. It is precisely this quality of daily life which makes the figures so unmistakably expressive. They do not transmit any personal gestures or manners, rather they show a pattern depersonalized but tremendously real, coming from everyday existence, hence their unity, their conclusive character. These conventional images of human figures reveal, with their gestures and actions, the vivacity of everyday occurrences.

It is clear that, in the broad region of West Mexico where the shaft tombs are found, in which the aforementioned terra-cottas were placed as offerings, there are also regional and local styles whose shared features demonstrate moments of great cultural integration. Among these styles, represented in this exhibition, I will highlight two because they have the most visual impact. One manifests itself in the shape of the warrior with the heavy body, solid shapeless legs, and short narrow arms that cross to take in their hands the object—a lance—that identifies the man *(Plate 4)*. The markedly deformed head exaggerates the extension, already elongated vertically, of the face to the point at which the head and the face seem to become excessively prolonged. But it is in this excessive lengthening, decidedly anti-natural, that the most notable characteristic and most expressive accent reside. The naive lack of natural proportions without a doubt gives the figure a decidedly conventional character, but it is in the facial expression, composed of the elliptic shapes of the eyes and mouth that integrate into a larger ellipse, and the vigorous attitude of the arms holding the weapon, where the strong will of the warrior's character is perceived.

One style different from the others in the Shaft Tomb area of West Mexico is that of the figures popularly known as "Chinescas" because of their seemingly Oriental facial features *(Plate 37)*. They are all female, with flat synthesized bodies, half-open legs that reveal their sex, and frequently—like the one shown here—they rest their faces in one hand. This confers an expression of profound thought or moving sadness. The head is wide and flat. There is no separation between the head and the forehead, the eyebrows are small curved reliefs and the eyes are small horizontal incisions in the middle of raised eyelids. The mouth is discreetly opened and the nose is fine and pointed. The treatment of such features is not casual; they are there because the ceramic sculptors made them and wanted them to have a different appearance from those manufactured by other communities and wanted also to endow the group with its own exclusive message. In spite of the differences, the formal model that unifies them all is evident; hence their conventional character. But it is, above all, their expression of deep dejection which makes the "Chinescas" a truly exceptional group.

Another mode of expression in the human figures of West Mexico should be remembered: that which alludes not to social conditions or spiritual states, but which present the physical nature of human disease. There is an abundance of hunchbacks—who are attributed with magic powers—and other figures who are deformed or have visible signs of injury or alteration of the skin, eyes, and lips. By showing these states of the body, the fragility of the human condition is explicitly expressed.

The Teotihuacan style, as seen in architecture, sculpture, painting, and ceramics, reveals startling homogeneity. This is the most vigorous, most defined, most totally unmistakable style. It has been said, truthfully, that an artistic will in which geometric and abstract shapes predominate determines the style, and the Teotihuacan objects exhibited here verify this.

The prototype of the conventional Teotihuacan face is the mask condensed into geometrical patterns. The tendency to accentuate the horizontality of the features becomes a distinctive formal attribute and contributes to the characteristic expression of controlled tension, serene and peaceful.

The synthesis of the features into geometric forms generalizes the faces; the parts are recognizable but the individual is absent. The flat foreheads extend like strips; the arches of the eyebrows describe almost straight lines; the eyes are represented schematically by lines that profile the cavities in spaces that follow horizontal edge of the figure, and in this same way the mouth is made up of fine, thin lips. In general the Teotihuacan face is one that concentrates, in a very defined way, its expressive qualities, which reveal striking correspondence with its formal qualities. Linear facial features underscore different planes of the face, inscribed in the outline of a trapezoid whose larger base corresponds with the upper limit of the forehead.

When the Teotihuacan tradition of a perfect and immutable order was established, the prototype was defined by and manifested in the arts, among them the characteristic figurines. Females are dressed in *quechquemitl* and skirt, and an enormous hat extending horizontally (*Plates* 56, 57, 58). There exists also the so-called "portrait type" which are actually portraits of the Teotihuacan prototype. Here there are no variations. The image can be mobile—by means of articulated extremities (*Plate* 22), or by being at the center of architectonic slabs of clay attached to an incense burner (*Plate* 86)—but the mode of representation does not change. If the geometric shapes, the symmetrical planes, the linear agreement, reveal an ordered composition of the cosmos, we must think, based on their artistic expressions, that the Teotihuacans (whose true name we do not know) had achieved a complete vision of their world in which all of its components had a precise place and a function to fulfill. The synthesis present in both the clothed and unclothed figures and the accentuated will to form in the immaterial faces communicate, it seems to me, an understanding of solidarity with the universe. The deep Teotihuacan religiosity annihilated the desire to express individuality in the representations, but it also integrated the most powerful Mesoamerican community and determined a mode of artistic production, a style, that would govern for several centuries (from the second to the eighth) in Mesoamerican history.

BY THE NINTH CENTURY the Toltecs, people who spoke Nahuatl, were established in Tula and their artistic style permeated a wide part of Mesoamerica, from the north and west down to the lowlands of the northern regions of the Mayan world. I will not delve deeply into the complicated problem that speaking of the "Toltec style" presupposes; I will limit myself to mentioning some of their most representative qualities without emphasizing the geographic and cultural origins of the objects considered here in the exhibition.

Among the Toltec sculptures that impart unequalled character to the Post-Classic imagery are the Atlantean figures, the standard bearers and the Chac Mools. Atlantean figures are the stone sculptures that are distinguished by hands raised high in the act of holding something (indeed, they are holding thick stone slabs, *Plate* 6). Their postures and faces are hieratic, compact and depersonalized; they are the anonymous expression of the warring community.

The standard bearers, a sculptural category that was perhaps created in the Epi-Classic period, are also emotionally inexpressive figures (*Plate* 5). Their rigid composition guards the objective of their representation to give form and presence, by means of an archetype, to the figure that symbolizes—generally—the image that must sustain the insignias of the society or the corporate group that it represented.

Chac Mools (this is simply a name which has been given to this sculptural genre) are semi-reclining human figures who hold plates over their bellies (*Plate* 20). In the Tarascan Chac Mool that is exhibited here, the synthesized shapes are squeezed into elemental geometric outlines, so the legs and arms are folded at an angle and the enormous hands open in a triangular arrangement. The deindividualized face is turned in the opposite direction of the body, the facial features charging the terrible, anodyne expression of anonymity.

Other figures of different ages—children, young women and men, elders—and different social conditions—warriors, women grinding corn—show the same intention of not expressing the individual entity. What matters is expressing their integration with the community, putting their personal lives in second place. The human is an instrument of social, political, and religious forces; his existence is recognized as being part of a group; and through representation of a prototype, a dynamic communion is founded among the members of a group. Humans do not conceive of themselves as different from other people and separated from nature. So for this reason, the faces of these genres of Pre-Hispanic sculptures are depersonalized, in spite of the fact that the features occasionally do not possess any noticeably great distance from the natural model.

THE PERSONALIZED EFFIGY

Among the human figures in the Pre-Hispanic plastic arts there are many that are portraits in the traditional sense of the term. I am referring to the representation of an individual, whether living or dead, real or imaginary, by means of interpreting moral or physical features. Even if there are other concepts of the portrait, for now I will abide by the idea that the portrait—the sculpted, painted, or modeled image—demands a degree of similarity with the model. In the Pre-Hispanic world there are images that reveal notable physical similarity to the model and that express various spiritual states, and there are others that are idealized effigies that go beyond the actual image.

Cultural, geographical and temporal circumstances favored an interest in reproducing the images of individuals who for certain reasons were distinguished in the community. The representation of priests, governors, military leaders, noble women, powerful men, and prisoners or illustrious prisoners demonstrates concretely the relationships of the individual with persons of distinct hierarchy and level. Nevertheless, not all of the Mesoamerican cultures gained consciousness of the development of man in his earthly sphere: the Olmecs, the Mayas and the peoples of the Classic Central Veracruz culture reveal in the artistic development of the portrait a dimension closer to the consciousness of nature. In the figures portrayed in this exhibition the degree of similitude varies. However, in all of them we can distinguish the image of the human as a creature who knows himself, who knows what he feels and does, of internal wisdom and of the external Nature. It is the human who orders and governs and is, in sum, nature's most superior being.

It is precisely this being—rational, sure of himself and dominant in the universe that he inhabits—who can be recognized in the objects presented in this exhibition. This human is seen in the Olmec figure, the terracottas from the center of Veracruz, the figurines from Jaina, in the stucco Maya profile, in the Zapotec urn with the female image, and in masks and statues carved by the Aztecs (*Plates 75, 10, 49, 64, 35, 26, 25, 24, 27, 29, 16, 7, 1, 9, 14, 50, 61, 66, 84*).

In the wide range of portraits bearing the seal of the style that overlaps them, there are some which stand out for the diligent reproduction of the model, for the emotions that they reveal, for the moral strength that they represent. As an example of the imitation of a model, we find exhibited here the sober Maya profile made of stucco (*Plate 16*). The source of the style comes from the region of Usumacinta, and it must have formed part of the decoration of some temple frieze or roofcomb. The Maya facial features are unmistakable: a flat forehead due to cranial deformation, a prominent nose curved by the addition of a plate that especially defines the profile, wide eyes split in half by drooping lids, a thin-lipped mouth, and a receding chin. The mark of time has not destroyed these features reproduced with honest clarity that hides nothing: the signs of age, the force of character, the wisdom attained, the experienced concentration are all present.

The figurines found as funeral offerings on the island of Jaina, in Campeche, are made of terracotta. All small in size, they make up the widest gallery of portraits in the Mesoamerican world. Among them are perceived persons of differing rank, condition and age, and in various activities and situations. In some of the figurines—the old woman and the weaver—the intensity of expression is astonishing (*Plates 64 and 60*). All of these images give testimony of the daily life of men, women, and children; hence their great freedom of expression. This is not about the "official" art of buildings and monuments, but rather small masterpieces created by local ceramicists.

Their variety suggests humanity seeking an identity in relation to others and in its daily toils. In this way, we see the countenance of the arrogant noble man, disdainful and well aware of his power (*Plate 26*); the face of the thinker who is meditating; the loved ones meeting each other (*Plate 35*); the solitary old woman with an energetic expression (*Plate 64*). They are all full of vitality and they recreate, in their fragile and carefully finished forms, real life in its natural daily condition.

I MUST MAKE a final mention, in the section on portrait art, of the Aztec effigies. They are, in great part, cut from stone and are products of the different workshops of these people, exceptional for their vigorous youthfulness, for their freshness and their sensible solutions to the challenges of existence, for their military rigor, for their decided will to survive. Although the Aztecs arrived late on the scene of Mesoamerican history, their achievements condense and establish the wisdom of centuries. Of particular physical typology, their stone images show that they are distinct from all those of Mesoamerica due to the strength of their features, their powerful expressions, their earthly authority. The mask *(Plate 85)*, the head of the dead man *(Plate 66)* and the other sculptures of Aztec men tell of this. The majestic and eloquent figure of the standard bearer who bids welcome to this exhibition certainly stands out among the above mentioned figures *(Plate 1)*. His individual physiognomy is perpetuated in the enlivened spirit behind the stone. In this effigy is perceived the consciousness that this man had of himself and his governing relationship with nature.

THE SUPERNATURAL IMAGE: ANTHROPOMORPHIC AND FANTASTIC

There are images that go beyond earthly nature. The symbolic attributes that these images show or the combination of different vital forms (anthropozoomorphic) with imaginary features point to their supernatural condition. These do not attempt to show lifelike expression, sentiments, or the spirit of the community. Rather, they achieve a reality which is not apprehended as such within perceivable nature. And although the figures of men and women may retain a similarity to nature—there is always a variable degree of anthropomorphism—the stylization, distortion, or superimposition of features imparts to them a certain symbolic quality. The supernatural character of the image is seen most clearly when the divinity is ascribed with botanical, terrestrial, or fantastic features. Natural elements taken from the animal or vegetable world or from the vast scope of the imagination clearly point out that the deity exhibiting these features enjoys a different mode of being than humans. In short, the deities—the supernatural—can be observed in the Pre-Hispanic plastic arts both in the lifelike representations, perhaps transfigured from the visual fact, and in the fantastic images having nothing in nature to which they can be compared. They are ways of expressing the human's meeting with the divine realm. On the one hand, there exist manifestations which uncover the sacred meaning of the cosmos; on the other hand, there are demonstrations of divine figures in concrete forms. It is fitting to explain that the images of supernatural beings do have a human structure, apparent or hidden, but recognizable. Only a few exceptions depart excessively from anthropomorphism.

THERE ARE FIGURES of gods, of diverse natures, who are represented with human features, and we will see some examples in this exhibition. On the one hand, there is the face on the ceremonial axe from the center of Veracruz that reproduces the conventional physiognomy of a man with bulging eyes, apparently closed, and chubby, hanging cheeks *(Plate 18)*. These are the anthropocentric features of a deity related symbolically to the ritual ball game. That is why it forms part of the representation of the axe, which is in turn a stone symbol of the belt used by the participants in this ritual.

There are two Aztec representations on exhibit here which relate to death. One is simply the cranium that is partially wasted away *(Plate 67)*, the other is an extremely beautiful sculpture of the goddess *Cihuateteo* who is kneeling over an altar decorated with skulls in relief *(Plate 68)*. There is no doubt that the manifestations in the Aztec plastic arts that repeat the physical characteristics of death relate to her, express her. But they express death in a singularly meaningful way. In no case is there ever a copy of a skull, although in essence it is reproduced in an image shown here that combines real elements with invented elements. This image is devoid of skin and flesh, and around the mouth it appears as if the skin were raised up. The skull has two rounded bulky objects in place of eyes, whereas in the representation of the goddess, the eyes are a flat circular surface. In fact, it seems that in both—and here we can generalize—what is important is the expression of the end of one cycle of life and the initiation of another. This is why there seems to be a process of regeneration; it is as if the figure were regaining its flesh, as if it were resuscitating. So it makes sense, then, that the bone be partially covered, because it expresses supernatural life. In this way, by uniting two very real things—life and death—the supernatural image acquires its true sense. To integrate that which in principle is different is to restore, to reconstitute the being in its original harmony.

The supernatural manifests itself in sculptural images in fantastic ways that range from a simple disguise that confers an identity—an eagle, a serpent, a jaguar, among others—to the distortion of features or the substitution of elements belonging to other creatures. The supernatural also appears when external elements are superimposed or combined to the extent that they are transfigured into something not recognizable from the natural world. This is, it seems to me, the most existential expression of a human in relation to the divine: that which is foreign to his physical perception, but natural to his spiritual position. It is a perceptive relationship in which an artist undertakes to make concrete an intellectual abstraction.

Due to the fact that the theme is covered in another chapter of this book, I will only mention that among the West Mexican shaft tomb sculptures, and those from the Gulf Coast, Maya, Zapotec, and Mexica, included in this exhibition, are human figures which are disguised, invented, imagined, that refer to a universe that is based upon a humanized god or a man with divine implications. The human figure is a resource used to express another nature. Its transfiguration can be explicit as in the case of the Aztec jaguar warrior *(Plate 9)*. And it can also be less evident, as occurs with the so-called priest who adopts a supernatural element by having his human head substituted by the head of an opossum *(Plate 70)*, or with that of the fat dog from the Shaft Tombs which is exhibited with a human mask *(Plate 74)*.

Sometimes we arrive at extreme cases in which divine expression is established through the perfect harmony of seven serpents that take the place of the head connected by the so-called neck, with the human body from which they raise in the renamed Tablet of Aparicio *(Plate 72)* and in abstractions from visible reality which are even greater. This is the case, for example, with the sun god in the clay cylinder which comes from Palenque *(Plate 73)*; in it we can still recognize anthropomorphic features which are concealed by signs referring to another reality, a supernatural reality.

IT IS THE HUMAN CONDITION and its relationship with nature which determine the different modes of perception and the varieties in its representation. Every one of these varying modes expresses differences inherent in human beings: when they reside in unending harmony with nature, when they shape a community that attempts to provide union at the same time as it is distancing itself from nature, when the separation from nature is initiated because of human penetration into the realm of self-knowledge and historical development. Also characteristic of human beings is the consciousness of the meeting with the divine, which is expressed with varying intensity and through diverse modes in Pre-Hispanic art. In these figures, anthropomorphic or fantastic, the power of putting oneself in contact with the divine can be clearly observed. In the expression of such representations, the being who is conscious of his superior nature can be recognized. Hence, his separation from that which is natural and visible and the association of elements that are only combined amongst themselves to form that which is above humanity, that which is beyond it.

The human who is transfigured acquires, both in his countenance and in his disguises, the magic power of controlling the nature which he inhabits. For this reason his human or divine expression becomes immutable.

BIBLIOGRAPHY

ALVERS, SVETLANA. "Style is What You Make of It: The Visual Arts Once Again," in *The Concept of Style*. Ithaca: Cornell University Press, 1987: 137-63.

FUENTE, BEATRIZ DE LA. *Peldaños en la conciencia: Rostros en la plástica prehispánica*. Universidad Autónoma de México, Art Collection No. 39, 2nd ed. 1985.

SOLÍS, FELIPE. *Gloria y Fama Mexica*. Smurfit Carton y Papel de México, S.A. de C.V. México 1991.

WÖLFFLIN, HEINRICH. *Conceptos Fundamentales de la Historia del Arte*. Madrid: Espasa-Calpe, 1985.

POLITICAL ORGANIZATION AND ARTISTIC EXPRESSION IN ANCIENT MEXICO

FELIPE SOLÍS

The inhabitants of ancient Mexico, like those of all communities that developed into civilizations with a distinctive character, created artistic expressions unique to them and that identify them. It is interesting to note that as these societies became more complex, incorporating political structures that led to a hierarchical state, their sculptural expression related or summarized itself in styles predetermined by specialists; essentially, the greater the sociopolitical complexity, the greater the complexity and rigidity of the characteristics that made up the artistic styles. These, then, permit the establishment of a clear difference between the sculptural art of the village or pre-state societies and those which reached a level of high political hierarchy.

We know from archaeological studies that around the year 2500 B.C. there emerged the first villages in Mesoamerican territory in which we are able to distinguish a mixed economy that would gradually, with the passage of time, base itself on intensive agriculture (Porter 1993: 25-52). To this level of economic development, there corresponds a social organization of certain complexity. The political leadership probably depended on the counsel of elders who would share their authority with the shamans or sorcerers. With this frame of reference, the artists of the pre-state societies created a multitude of images whose dominant formal model was that of nude women who on occasion were dressed with simple wraps that are used as small skirts or pants *(Plates 30, 31, 32, 33)*. The nudity as an element contrasts with the women's ornate hair styles and adornments including the abundant jewelry of the era, among which are common necklaces, ear ornaments, and bracelets in great quantity (Covarrubias 1961: 26).

These diminutive sculptures were created individually using techniques such as modeling, incision, and pastiche. The artist highlighted the ornamental detail that was then in style: body and facial make-up achieved with red, white, or yellow lines like those present in many of these figurines (Ibid: 30).

While it is possible to talk about the tradition of these feminine figurines as a fundamental artistic expression of the Pre-Classic period, we also find—although in very small quantity—images of shamans or sorcerers identifiable by their complicated headdresses, the masculine clothing that reminds us of the *maxtlatl* of later eras and the masks covering their faces (Ibid: 28). There are also representations of the male ball players (Piña Chán 1955: 39-40) and some scenes in which two people are found in a discursive position seated on a bench of great proportions (Ibid: 29).

As mentioned above, there is little evidence of control by the leaders on the massive production of these small sculptures; rather, there seems to have been great liberty in terms of creativity. The basic norm may have consisted of defining the feminine based on nudity, defining the fertility of the woman through pregnancy, and what we could understand as an expression of femininity exaggerating the narrowness of the waist and the volume of the thighs and legs; the masculine may have been defined by the clothing covering the genitals and by the distinctive activity of the men of that time which was basically their participation in rites and ceremonies.

There is also great freedom in terms of the positions and expressions of the clay figures in this group. The majority of the women are standing up and facing forward, though some are seated, reclining, or suckling children and dogs, accompanying their babies in cribs, and even enacting complicated dance postures. The masculine sculptures are standing up or performing complex and difficult contortions.

We will conclude that the large contingent of anthropomorphic images, both male and female, recreates with great liberty the dominant social reality of early village life. The most significant examples, and the best known, originate from the formative or Pre-Classic sites excavated in the Mexican Central High Plateau from which Tlatilco has provided the greatest number of pieces and in which we can also appreciate the richest thematic group.

In West Mexico, a culture was developed that extended itself from the State of Michoacan to the State of

Nayarit and which is commonly known as the Shaft Tomb culture. They excavated into the subsoil of very compact earth, distinctive hollow tombs connected to the surface by shafts that remind us of wells. In these subterranean cavities they would deposit their dead, accompanying them with many rich offerings among which stand out mostly hollow, attractive clay sculptures that on occasion served as receptacles. Among Shaft Tomb sculptures are also numerous representations of familiar animals that figure among the most vivid and realistic testimonials of Mexican Pre-Hispanic art. For the sake of remembering we will mention the famous fat dogs of Colima *(Plate 74)*. (Solís 1991: 180-181). But focusing on the theme of our exhibition, the anthropomorphic figures, it is truly important that through West Mexican sculpture we are able to penetrate more deeply into the most intimate details of the daily life of that region. This is due principally to the fact that this Shaft Tomb culture did not develop into complex state organizations as did cultures at the same time or later (A.D. 300-800) in other Mesoamerican regions. In the High Central Plateau, Teotihuacan stands out, as do cities of the Oaxaca region and the Maya world.

FOR SOME TIME NOW, students of New World Pre-Columbian art have found a curious parallel between early village art and that of the Shaft Tomb culture. The latter is recognized for the freshness and spontaneity, as well as the realism, that the ceramicists gave their creations. In all the figures of West Mexico, these elements are present. In this manner we have the hunchbacks or sick that crudely recount with great realism the pains and deformities with which they lived *(Plates 78, 80, 81)*. Also present are the proud warriors who brandish their offensive and defensive weapons *(Plate 4)*, the women that suckle their children *(Plate 54)*, the matrons that are the prototype of the model of beauty and the feminine requirement of that time expressed as robust body, wide hips, and protruding breasts, all of which served to announce the woman's fertility and the abundance of nourishment for her children *(Plates 17, 62)*.

In this art of West Mexico are images of the family in which the father, mother, and children enjoy intimate contact and the pleasures of life's everyday happy moments *(Figures 47, 48*; Baus y Flores 1990: 257-293).

We have already mentioned the fat dogs of Colima, of which many examples are known, including one that wears a human mask *(Plate 74)*. It points to the intention of the artist to associate the funny canine with the destiny of man. In the mythological tales of some of the Mesoamerican peoples, it is mentioned that the dog—called by Nahuatl speakers *itzcuintli*—was the animal in charge of guiding the souls of the deceased to Mictlan, the kingdom of the dead, located in the Underworld. This required the sacrifice of a dog during the funeral ceremonies so that when the spirit of the deceased arrived at the edge of a subterranean river called Chignahuapan after having surpassed numerous dangers on the trip through the nine inferior planes, the human spirit would find the spirit of the dog, which would help the deceased cross the river, enabling him to reach his final destination: the dark place where Mictlantechuhtli, the lord of the dead, ruled.

In a central area of the Gulf Coast region, in a period that ranges from 1200 to 600 B.C., the Olmec culture was developed, living alongside numerous rural societies. The evolution of Olmec culture developed into complex political and social systems that to this date are a subject of debate: some researchers consider that among the Olmecs are found the seeds of the earliest Mesoamerican state.

When we approach the rich collection of artistic expressions produced by the Olmecs, we immediately find ourselves with an art that contrasts with that of other cultures from this Formative period. Those inhabitants of the southern region of Veracruz and western Tabasco built important ceremonial centers such as La Venta, San Lorenzo, Tres Zapotes, etc., where monumental architecture can be found, and whose buildings were distributed according to predetermined models of construction with constant astronomical orientation.

The Olmecs' most significant sculptural expressions were carved from volcanic rocks. From this great collection human figures stand out. Among these we have the famous colossal heads, the anthropomorphic and mythical anthropomorphic sculptures, the stelae, monumental altars and receptacles (De la Fuente 1973).

In this sculptural complex, a formal and iconographic model distinguishes itself. Out of necessity it responds to a complex social and political organization, in which existed not only a clearly differentiated division of classes, but also of ranks within the leadership. The latter controlled these ceremonial centers and their population, they organized the rites and assured the selection of the proper ritual paraphernalia. But most importantly, this leadership systematized the elements or basic traits of their symbolic language which, when molded or engraved onto stone or mud, allowed the viewer of those messages to recognize a basic pattern of communication —one that unified the population with the ideals of leadership. Everyone recognized himself as an integral part of a greater organization made up of the leaders, chiefs and priests, traders, artisans, agricultural laborers, etc. All were able, through this language of complex but systematic forms, to identify themselves both ethnically and culturally.

Art, then, as a product of a social organization that tends to levels of complexity, had as its mission societal cohesion. These artistic manifestations, by forming a part of the ideological apparatus of the state, repress and control the creative liberty of those indigenous artists who, in a coerced manner, have to obey and respect the visual canons of imagery and style that the political hierarchy establishes. Through the unification of this artistic language, there is a constant in the messages: the formal and iconographic models which allow the state to transmit the communication to society as a whole, and to the diverse parts of the whole. It is undeniable that there can be many different readings of these messages, but in the end, all the elements that make up the cultural entirety of a state society give to the people the sense of integration that the state wants expressed (*Plate 75*).

We are able to recognize these principles of art not only among the Olmecs, but also in other cultures that, as of the third and fourth century of our era, developed in the Mesoamerican region. In the Mexican High Central Plateau, the extraordinary city of Teotihuacan dominated all others. In its moment of splendor, around A.D. 500, it created artistic models that defined a clearly recognizable style. The Teotihuacans had reached an equilibrium, chiefly in architecture, that even to this day surprises us by its combination of slopes and projecting panels that give that indigenous capital a special magnificence of character.

The human figure is also integrated harmoniously with the architectural whole, captured in the numerous murals that decorated the majority of the living spaces of the ceremonial buildings. The painters had conformed to create depictions of men and women of different positions and expressions combined with representations of the deities and of real or fantastic flora and fauna, thus giving the entire composition a sacred and symbolic character.

In Teotihuacan stone sculpture there has been conserved, in definite recognizable forms, the presence of man and the concept of that which is human in direct relation to the city and its urban character. One of these is the great monolith known as Chalchiuhtlicue, a unique piece which presents itself to us as a standing woman made up of the following elements: head, torso, skirt, and feet. They were conceived by their creators as interrelating geometrical forms of primary character that give the illusion of a single architectural structure.

As George Kubler has posited, that piece could have served as an architectural support like a gigantic anthropomorphic column (Kubler 1989:60), an antecedent, perhaps, of the known caryatids or Atlantean figures of Tula and Chichén. What that sculpture communicates to us is that this stone figure should not be differentiated from the great urban whole. Rather, its representation should be integrated harmoniously to it whether in the murals or as an architectural form.

Another sculptural group in which the human element is recognizable is the *huehueteotl*—ceremonial urns consisting of a seated individual, bent over with his legs crossed, holding atop his head and back a receptacle. All these figures—certainly the large number which were discovered in Teotihuacan—repeat the same pattern in terms of the position and especially the sex and age of the person. They are of older men whose decrepitude is expressed on the face covered by wrinkles with only their eye teeth remaining, having lost their incisors due to advanced age. These sculptures, like the great Chalchiuhtlicue, were designed as geometric forms that superimpose themselves over each other and remind us in some way of the profiles of the Teotihuacan buildings that make up the already mentioned combination of slopes and projecting panels.

The influence that Teotihuacan had on other Mesoamerican regions can be detected by the presence of these artistic patterns. They were taken to distant lands either by commercial exchange or religious or militaristic campaigns. When these elements were copied according to the original patterns or canons, they made the creators of these imitations not only feel in style but also closer to the great city that dictated both the style of life and thought.

Even in the small Teotihuacan figurines made from clay we can recognize the formal and stylistic patterns that contrast definitely with the ceramic art of the village cultures that preceded them (*Plates 65, 56, 57, 58, 55, 86, 87, 22*). In the earliest moments of Teotihuacan, the diminutive sculptures were made by modeling them and achieving their decorative details through incision and the use of pastiche, later adding decorative details with brilliant colors. Some centuries later, this technique was superceded by the use of molds which permitted the artisans to produce en masse thousands of these representations.

The figurines of Teotihuacan fit into completely schematic groups in which the positions, expressions, and clothing are repeated. This shows us that this ceramic art also responds definitively to the canons established by the political hierarchy of Teotihuacan. In these canons, the creative freedom of the ceramicist is reduced to the creation of higher quality molds which permit the faithful reproduction of the original model previously defined.

We will lastly focus our attention on the analysis of artistic objects that were produced in the era of the Aztec, and in particular those which originate from the capital city, México-Tenochtitlan.

The ancestors of the Aztec were the Toltecs and other peoples who lived in different areas of the Mexican High Central Plateau between 1300 B.C. and A.D. 1000. It was the residents of Tula who in reality had the greatest significance in historical, cultural, and artistic terms for the founders of Tenochtitlan.

The Toltecs created in the Mexican High Central Plateau an artistic style that probably originated in the Maya world of the Yucatan Peninsula. In the Toltec artistic tradition the human figure takes on a unique presence with a representative force that has only the Olmec era as a point of comparison. Basically, the sculptures represent individuals of the male sex. Their presence reached a monumental character in the caryatids and Atlantean figures discovered by Jorge R. Acosta during his excavations in the city of Quetzalcoatl. There we have authentic anthropomorphic columns in which we can distinguish warriors in all their finery that by their physical presence are the actual support of the temple of the most important deity.

Those men, wrought in stone, are presented to us also as smaller Atlantean figures that lift their hands in a position to help support the weight atop their heads *(Plate 6)*. We also have individuals, either seated or standing, with hands placed in a certain manner to hold flags or standards, for which reason we call them standard bearers *(Plates 1, 5)*. It was in Tula, in the Mexican High Central Plateau, where the image of the reclining man lying on his back in a difficult position was fixed as a model. On this reclining man's stomach there was a type of plate or the base of a receptacle. We refer to the figure called Chac Mool that certainly had as its purpose to serve as an altar or sacrificial stone in the Toltec-related ceremonial complex in Michoacan *(Plate 20)*.

This anthropomorphic sculpture and all the other groups, stone stelae, etc., in which jaguars, eagles, coyotes, etc., are present, respond positively to the political structure and the character of Toltec society where war is the tonic of the moment. The battles and military conquests correspond to these images of warriors that communicate to the community as a whole a sense of pride that would permit them to form a part of a militaristic state as Tula must have been in its time.

According to the historical traditions, the Aztec founded their capital city in the year A.D. 1325 and they themselves describe for us their modest origins. But their ability with weapons and their messianic character take them to the imposition of their will over other peoples through conquest and domination thus imposing upon them the necessity to pay tribute either by work or in kind.

The art of the city of Huitzilopochtli (Tenochtitlan), like that of Teotihuacan or Tula, responds to the state's apparatus. In this era, there no longer remain the traces of inventiveness and free creativity of the artists and artisans. These now follow the canons and outlines of an iconographic program and of an absolutely rigid representational system.

The human figure is fundamentally expressed using volcanic rocks such as andesite and basalt, that because of their hardness, assured permanence. As we have stated above, it is possible to classify this sculptural production into clearly differentiated subjects or genres (Solís, 1982).

For the ruling Aztec apparatus, it was important to differentiate the distinct positions and attitudes that men and women should have. As seen through sculpture this should not be only a reflection of what was happening in society. By the same token, clothing, adornments, and headdresses can be classified according to the sex of the figures. We already know that in México-Tenochtitlan the external elements such as clothes, hair styles, jewelry, etc., served as a way of immediately identifying not only the sex of the person but also their position in the hierarchy and the role they played in society.

Even more so, the majority of the representations that we preserve from these people shows us individuals beautifully clad. Nudity was a socially punishable act and the few known nude figures must have been associated with fertility and were probably never exhibited publicly as for example the phallic adolescent *(Plate 50;* Solís 1991: 233) or the nude woman originating from Texcoco (Ibid: 234).

The same is true for the multiple-figure sculptures. We know of only one Aztec sculpture in which two individuals of the opposite sex touch each other or embrace *(Plate 34)*. This is a clear reference to the sexual act, for which reason the faces of the persons have been changed to those of monkeys accentuating the libidinousness of the representation. For the Aztec state, sexual unrestraint was not only reprehensible but also punishable by death. For this reason art does not sponsor or popularize such actions. The existence of the Aztec Couple is owed probably to the ritual requiring the representation of the original couple Ometecuhctli-Omecihuatl, from which not only did humanity originate but also the pantheon of the Aztec; since they were in an eternal sexual embrace they were so represented (Solís 1992).

Aztec society considered itself the definitive representative of the populations of the Fifth Creation, the most recent, which was illuminated by the Fifth Sun. Since they considered themselves the superior and best designed series of humans, they portrayed themselves in the ideal condition of eternal youth. Even the wrinkles on the images of the old god or *huehueteotl* were erased, only maintaining the presence of the long eyeteeth, as they had been conceived of in Teotihuacan sculpture.

This community, followers of the Tezcatlipoca and Huitzilopochtli, the gods of war par excellence, exalted youth, especially males for their disposition for war and braveness, established them as the pattern of idealized conduct. The women needed to be like the goddesses of fertility, always ready to have more children and to contribute with their effort and work to the maintenance of home and family.

The art of that time, as expressed through magnificent sculptures or diminutive clay figurines, shows us a society whose ideals of survival and dominion over nature were fixed by the state apparatus of the Aztec. They imposed a model for the citizen whose conduct should be followed by the entire community. This model lasted until its destruction during the European conquest occurring at the beginning of the sixteenth century.

1

2

4

5

6

7

42

8

9

44

10

11

12

13

14

15

16

17

18

19

20

21

22

23

24

25

26

27

28

29

30

31

66

32

33

68

34

35

36

37

38

39

40

41

76

42

43

44

45

46

47

48

49

84

50

51

52

53

54

55

56

57

58

59

60

61

62

64

65

66

67

68

69

104

70

71

72

73

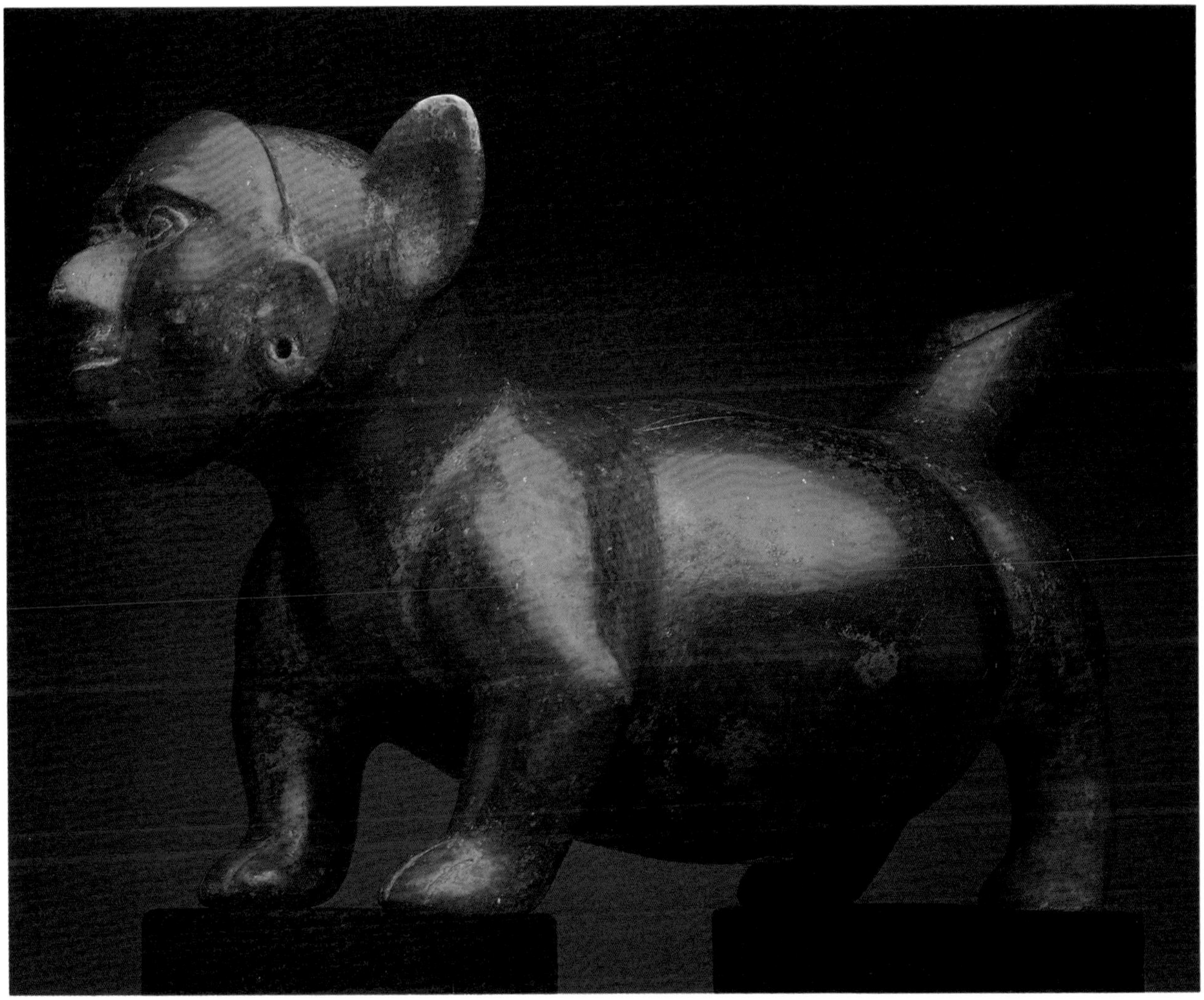

74

75

76

77

78

79

80

81

82

83

118

84

85

120

86

87

88

89

90

91

92

CATALOGUE ENTRIES

MARI CARMEN SERRA PUCHE
and FELIP SOLÍS

1. YOUNG MAN

This sculpture, which represents a young Aztec man, is the most beautiful and most finely finished specimen bequeathed to us by that culture. The details of his anatomy and the careful treatment of his characterstic garment, the máxtlatl, indicate that the piece was sculpted by a master stone-cutter.
Mexico City
Aztec
Late Post-Classic, A.D. 1300-1521
Stone
Height: 80 cm
Width: 28 cm

2. PRISONER

This vigorous sculpture represents a young Maya man with a deformed skull and the scarification that suggest a symbolic beard; although fragmented, the phallic character of the piece is unmistakable. He is popularly known as the adolescent from Kumpich.
Kumpich, State of Campeche
Maya
Early Post-Classic, A.D. 900-1220
Stone
Height: 98 cm
Width: 43 cm

3. HOLLOW BABY

The ceramic sculptures that identify the Olmec world are made by leaving the inside hollow; the one we observe here is one typical of this style. It shows an asexual, nude individual with an enigmatic face and characteristic eyes, wide nose and thick lips with a downturned mouth. The reddish hair stands out, unusual in these figures.
Provenience Unknown
Olmec
Pre-Classic, 1200-600 B.C.
Ceramic
Height: 25.4 cm
Width: 28.5 cm

4. WARRIOR FIGURE

In the shaft tombs of West Mexico numerous figures, believed to be warriors, have been discovered; in this example we observe one of these valiant individuals holding his weapon.
State of Nayarit
Shaft Tomb Culture
Proto-Classic, 200 B.C.-A.D. 200
Ceramic
Height: 73.5 cm
Width: 43.7 cm

5. STANDARD BEARER

This sculpture with the image of a Toltec warrior would be located in the upper section or platform of a building in Tula. In accordance with the position of the hands that form a hollow space, the function of this figure would be that of standard bearer or flag holder.
Tula, State of Hidalgo
Toltec
Early Post-Classic, A.D. 900-1250
Stone
Height: 1.07 cm
Width: 39 cm

6. ATLANTEAN FIGURE

In the Yucatan Peninsula, and specifically in the city of Chichén-Itzá, there abound sculptures called Atlantean figures. They were represented with raised arms and their function was to hold up pedestals or lintels. This piece represents a warrior who displays a pectoral adornment in the form of a stylized butterfly.
Chichén-Itzá, State of Yucatan.
Maya
Early Post-Classic, A.D. 900-1250
Stone
Height: 86.5 cm
Width: 50 cm

7. WOMAN

When we observe this clay sculpture of a Zapotec woman with her typical clothing, skirt and *quechquémitl*, and the coiffure that weaves the hair with cotton cords, we cannot but remember the present-day indigenous women of the Yalalag region, in Oaxaca, who wear similar adornment and attire.
Provenience Unknown
Zapotec
Classic, A.D. 300-900
Ceramic
Height: 34 cm
Width: 27.7 cm

8. PENSIVE MAN

This elegant figure modeled with great mastery shows us an individual who lightly rests his head on one arm, reflecting profound meditation.
State of Colima
Shaft Tomb Culture
Proto-Classic, 200 B.C.-A.D. 200
Ceramic
Height: 21.2 cm
Width: 21.3 cm

9. JAGUAR WARRIOR

The young people belonging to the Mexica, or Aztec, nobility formed military groups who had as an insignia the two most rapacious animals of those times: the eagle and the jaguar. It is precisely the image of one of these warriors that is presented in this sculpture; in it we can see a man with severe features who proudly wears a feline-shaped helmet; the pleated paper crest at the nape of the neck is the mark of nobility. The individual is seated on a throne and richly adorned with jewelry made of jade and precious metals.
Mexico City
Aztec
Late Post-Classic, A.D. 1300-1521
Stone
Height: 80 cm
Width: 47.3 cm

10. FEMALE FIGURE WITH RED PAINT

Some ceramic styles from the Veracruz region can be distinguished by the application of decorative designs through the utilization of intense red pigments. This is the case of these female figures in which the beauty and elegance of the women of those times stands out in the decoration.
El Faisan, State of Veracruz
Classic Central Veracruz Culture
Classic, A.D. 300-900
Ceramic
Height: 34.5 cm
Width: 29.1 cm

11. NUDE WOMAN

The potters from the Casas Grandes region, an archaeological site located near the northern border of Mexico, modeled pots in the form of humans, like this one that shows us a nude, seated woman. The entire body was decorated with geometric and symbolic designs in black and red on white clay.
Casas Grandes, State of Chihuahua
Casas Grandes
Late Post-Classic, A.D. 1060-1340
Ceramic
Height: 19.5 cm
Width: 17 cm

12. NUDE MAN

The vessels from Casas Grandes, besides presenting geometric designs painted in polychrome, are also animated by modeling of the clay, primarily in the form of slender seated men. In these vessels we can perceive the concept that those northern peoples had of the human body and its characteristics.
Casas Grandes, State of Chihuahua
Casas Grandes
Late Post-Classic, A.D. 1060-1340
Ceramic
Height: 20 cm
Width: 16 cm

13. RED WOMAN

Besides having ornamental details and features created with fine incision, Pre-Classic female figurines modeled in clay were also covered with paint indicating that in those times bodily and facial cosmetics were used. This hollow figure is distinguished for its enormous size and its brilliantly polished surface, which makes the red paint covering the piece all the more noticeable.
Tlatilco, State of Mexico
Middle Pre-Classic, 1200-800 B.C.
Ceramic
Height: 54.5 cm
Width: 17.2 cm

14. WARRIOR HEAD

In Tenochtitlan, a sculptural tradition was developed in which fired clay was carved. This warrior head is one notable example in which we observe the severe features that define the face of a victorious indigenous conquistador distinguished by the military ornament called *bezote* that was placed on the lower part of the lip, above the chin.
Mexico City
Aztec
Late Post-Classic, A.D. 1325-1521
Ceramic
Height: 19.1 cm
Width: 15.6 cm

15. POLYCHROME PLATE

Maya ceramics are among the most attractive of all Mesoamerican pottery, fundamentally because almost all of the known decorative techniques were used in its manufacture. In this polychrome plate can be seen a seated person, in which we recognize the characteristically deformed cranium, a practice of embellishment used by the Maya.
Provenience Unknown
Maya
Classic, A.D. 300-900
Ceramic
Height: 6.4 cm
Width: 28.4 cm

16. PROFILE

The Maya sculptors of the Classic period modeled, with great mastery, images, portraits of the outstanding members of society, using stucco as their material. In this fragment we can observe the realism with which the facial features were captured in the profile of a person whose prominent nose and deformed skull are accentuated by the hair style.
Palenque, State of Chiapas
Maya
Classic, A.D. 300-900
Stucco
Height: 15 cm
Width: 15 cm

17. WOMAN WITH SCARIFICATION

In this elegant sculpture modeled in clay we can observe a West Mexican woman seated on a bench, holding a plate in one hand. The decoration on her shoulders, called scarification, is a beauty practice used in ancient Mexico. She could be considered the ideal of femininity who gathers her family around her.
Provenience Unknown
Shaft Tomb Culture
Proto-Classic, 200 B.C.-A.D. 200
Ceramic
Height: 55 cm
Width: 30 cm

18. ANTHROPOMORPHIC AXE

Within the artistic manifestations of the cultures from Central Veracruz, the so-called ceremonial axes stand out. They are thought to be stylized heads of those decapitated in the ball game.

This sacrificial symbol shows us an obese individual with fat cheeks and a curious hairstyle in which one long lock runs from his forehead to the nape of his neck.
State of Veracruz
Classic Central Veracruz Culture
Classic, A.D. 300-900
Stone
Height: 18.7 cm
Width: 12.1 cm

19. WARRIOR HEAD

In the Yucatan Peninsula, sculptors took advantage of the calcareous stone to carve images of warriors who were distinguished in society by the use of ornaments and insignias. This warrior possesses a zoomorphic helmet and semicircular fan.
Uxmal, State of Yucatan
Maya
Late Classic, A.D. 700-900
Stone
Height: 32.5 cm
Width: 35 cm

20. CHAC-MOOL

The tradition of sculpted images of semi-reclining human figures who hold plates over their bellies and who are known by the name of Chac-Mool extended all the way to Michoacan. The Tarascan artists synthesized the individual's form in a combination of cubist geometry and human shape.
State of Michoacan
Tarascan
Late Post-Classic, A.D. 1300-1521
Stone
Height: 59 cm
Width: 80 cm

21. HEAD

The modeled clay figures from the center of Veracruz in the Classic period were elaborated with great realism; just by observing them we note the authentic features of those past ethnicities.

In this finely modeled head we can see the practice of facial embellishment that required dental mutilation and the utilization of "chapopote" (bitumen) to accentuate the distinctions of the hair or facial cosmetics.
Remojadas, Veracruz
Classic Central Veracruz Culture
Classic, A.D. 300-900
Ceramic
Height: 19 cm
Width: 23 cm

22. JOINTED DOLL

In about the sixth century of this era, the production of figurines made from molds was intensified; in this curious piece, the artisan independently manufactured the body and its extremities, joining them together later with vegetable fibers. Some researchers think that these dolls could be some kind of puppet, while others maintain that the mobility of the extremities was related to their ritual placement in funerary offerings.
Teotihuacan, State of Mexico
Teotihuacan
Classic, 100 B.C.-A.D. 600
Ceramic
Height: 29.7 cm
Width: 13.2 cm

23. NOBLE WOMAN

Confronted with these beautifully modeled clay figurines we get the impression of what it was like to admire Maya women of the past wearing their elegant textiles. We can identify here the skirt and long *huipil*, as well as the jewelry and complicated ornaments that adorn the woman's hairstyle.
Jaina, Campeche
Maya
Classic, A.D. 300-900
Ceramic
Height: 20.7 cm
Width: 9.1 cm

24. BALL PLAYER

Individuals who dedicated themselves to practicing ballplaying used knee and arm protection as well as a sort of voluminous belt that covered the waist, just like the one we see in this figurine. This person displays his headdress in the shape of a deer's head.
Jaina, State of Campeche
Maya
Classic, A.D. 300-900
Ceramic
Height: 21 cm
Width: 9 cm

25. GOVERNOR ON HIS THRONE

At the burial sites on the island of Jaina, numerous molded clay figurines that accompanied the dead as a form of symbolic offering have been discovered. It is supposed that they represented, in many instances, the activity or position of the person when he was alive, as in this case where we see a ruler seated in his palanquin, or litter.
Jaina, State of Campeche
Maya
Classic, A.D. 300-900
Ceramic
Height: 22.7 cm
Width: 11 cm

26. ARROGANT ONE

Mayas in the Campeche region had the custom of burying their dead on Jaina island, very close to the coast; the deceased were accompanied by magnificent offerings which are best known for their beautifully decorated clay figurines, like this one which represents a man wearing a false beard and who is identified by a large chest piece made of a sea shell.
Jaina, State of Campeche
Maya
Classic, A.D. 300-900
Ceramic
Height: 17.8 cm
Width: 8.8 cm

27. ELEGANT LADY

This ancient Maya woman displays elegant clothing that consists of a skirt and a garment that, like a blouse, covers her torso and arms, leaving her neckline exposed; the woman's rank is accented by the enormous necklace made of green beads and the hairstyle in which her profile and cranial deformation stand out.
Jaina, State of Campeche
Maya
Classic, A.D. 300-900
Ceramic
Height: 15.4 cm
Width: 9.6 cm

28. WARRIOR

The Maya artisans who molded ceramics were the artists who created the famous figurines from Jaina. In this piece we see a warrior wearing his woven cotton armor, holding a fan in one hand; the figurine still bears remnants of a particular paint called "Maya blue."
Jaina, State of Campeche
Maya
Classic, A.D. 300-900
Ceramic
Height: 14.8 cm
Width: 6.9 cm

29. FIGURE SEATED ON LEGS

The skill of the Maya artisans can be seen in the numerous clay molds in which various positions of life were represented and in which we generally observe young adults in the vital moment of their existence.
Jaina, State of Campeche
Maya
Classic, A.D. 300-900
Ceramic
Height: 13.7 cm
Width: 10 cm

30. "PRETTY LADY"

In the era of village cultures, the most important tradition consisted of modeling of nude feminine figures who were clearly associated with the fertility both of the woman herself and of the land, and which were used as agricultural amulets or talismans.
Tlatilco, State of Mexico
Pre-classic High Central Plateau
Pre-Classic, 1200-100 B.C.
Ceramic
Height: 9 cm
Width: 3.7 cm

31. "PRETTY LADY"

During the Pre-Classic period the feminine clay modeled figurines with images of nude women, besides having ornamental details and features which were achieved through fine incisions, were also covered with paint that indicated the facial and corporeal cosmetic practices of the times.
Tlatilco, State of Mexico
Pre-Classic High Central Plateau
Pre-Classic, 1200-100 B.C.
Ceramic
Height: 9.5 cm
Width: 3.4 cm

32. "PRETTY LADY"

The ideal of beauty among the village cultures is reflected in the female figurines in which a narrow waist, short thorax, small breasts, large hips, and voluminous thighs exalt the grace of nudity.
Tlatilco, State of Mexico
Pre-Classic High Central Plateau
Pre-Classic, 1200-100 B.C.
Ceramic
Height: 11.5 cm
Width: 5 cm

33. "PRETTY LADY"

The clay figurines from the Pre-Classic era are delicately modeled sculptures of small dimensions that show us the idealized form of feminine grace, in which there is an equilibrium between the nudity and the elegant hairstyle.
Tlatilco, State of Mexico
Pre-Classic High Central Plateau
Pre-Classic, 1200-100 B.C.
Ceramic
Height: 8.1 cm
Width: 3.5 cm

34. COUPLE
This unique sculpture shows a pair of individuals with monkey faces. The fact that each touches the other with their arms is a clear allusion to the sexual act, and this is why they have been identified as the image of the original couple in Aztec mythology, Ometecuhtli-Omecihuatl.
Mexico City
Aztec
Late Post-Classic, A.D. 1300-1521
Stone
Height: 38 cm
Width: 34.5 cm
Length: 40 cm

35. THE EMBRACE
In the Pre-Hispanic world, marriage was the fundamental act that initiated the adult life of men and women. There was a pre-established sequence of events that culminated in the ultimate encounter of the couple. This figurine evokes precisely that intimate act.
Jaina, State of Campeche
Maya
Classic, A.D. 400-800
Ceramic
Height: 12 cm
Width: 8.1 cm

36. THE CREATOR COUPLE
The contrast of the geometric with the sensual is magnificently represented in this vase. This unique piece tackles the topic of the openly represented sexual act, a theme not developed by the people of ancient Mexico, probably due to the repressive elements of their religious principles.
Casas Grandes, State of Chihuahua
Casas Grandes
Post-Classic, A.D. 900-1340
Ceramic
Height: 15.5 cm
Width: 17 cm

37. CHINESCA
The beautiful clay sculptures, with delicate features, among which are remarkable elongated eyes, are known by those who study West Mexican art as "Chinescas." This piece, without a doubt, is the most finely finished of all those we have encountered; we must appreciate the stupendous equilibrium the artist achieved in giving the figure this difficult position with her legs bent.
State of Nayarit
Shaft Tomb Culture
Proto-Classic, 200 B.C.-A.D. 200
Ceramic
Height: 31 cm
Width: 26 cm

38. PREGNANT WOMAN
The peasant groups of the Mexican central plateau placed great importance on pregnancy through numerous figurines representing its different stages.
Tlatilco, State of Mexico
Pre-Classic High Central Plateau
Pre-Classic, 1200-600 B.C.
Ceramic
Height: 8.4 cm
Width: 6.3 cm

39. PREGNANT WOMAN
With great realism the ceramicists of the village cultures recreated the look of pregnant women: prominent bellies and large breasts. In this figurine we note the final phase of pregnancy, foretelling the impending birth.
Tlatilco, State of Mexico
Pre-Classic High Central Plateau
Pre-Classic, 1200-600 B.C.
Ceramic
Height: 7.4 cm
Width: 5.5 cm

40. PREGNANT WOMAN
A woman's prime was reached during pregnancy, according to these peasant groups, and it was therefore represented with great realism. In this figurine we note the universal acceptance of woman's reproductive power, associated with the fertility of the land.
Tlatilco, State of Mexico
Pre-Classic High Central Plateau
Pre-Classic, 1200-600 B.C.
Ceramic
Height: 6.7 cm
Width: 3.5 cm

41. PREGNANT WOMAN
In the life cycle of agricultural peoples there is a clear association between the period of women's pregnancy and the season when the crops grow.
Tlatilco, State of Mexico
Pre-Classic High Central Plateau
Pre-Classic, 1200-600 B.C.
Ceramic
Height: 5.8 cm
Width: 3.5 cm

42. CHILD
The first stage of childhood in Aztec society was considered as a time of apprenticeship; in this figurine we have an infant seated in his wooden chair, waiting to be fed by his mother.
Tlatelolco, Mexico City
Aztec
Late Post-Classic, A.D. 1300-1521
Ceramic
Height: 8.2 cm
Width: 3.5 cm

43. HOLLOW BABY

In order to produce the hollow figures of the "baby face" tradition, potters used a fine brown clay which they modeled with great mastery; the person's features were achieved through shaping the clay and making incisions. In this figure there are still traces of the original paint.
Gualupita, State of Morelos
Pre-Classic High Central Plateau
Pre-Classic, 1200-100 B.C.
Clay
Height: 27 cm
Width: 21 cm

44. CRIB

In order to care for newborns parents manufactured a special piece of furniture carved from wood that is similar to the cribs of other cultures, except that they had a peculiar curved frame which allowed the child to be covered with a thin cloth.
Chupicuaro, Guanajuato
Chupicuaro
Pre-Classic, 400-100 B.C.
Ceramic
Height: 4.5 cm
Width: 3.8 cm
Length: 7.7 cm

45. CRIB

Sometimes in representations of babies in their cribs we also have the presence of mothers who lovingly care for them; this type of representation is found exclusively in the Pre-Classic or Formative period and considered characteristic of peasant art.
Chupicuaro, Guanajuato
Chupicuaro
Pre-Classic, 400-100 B.C.
Ceramic
Height: 4.3 cm
Width: 7.1 cm

46. CRIB

Through the various ethnohistoric versions, we know that in some of the Pre-Hispanic Mexican cultures babies in their cribs were given their official names just a few days after being born, the names being chosen through a complicated guessing game that involved different colored seeds.
Chupicuaro, Guanajuato
Chupicuaro
Pre-Classic, 400-100 B.C.
Ceramic
Height: 5.7 cm
Width: 5.5 cm

47. FAMILY

Many of the pieces from Colima reproduce aspects of daily life. This family scene, however, is exceptional; the father is seated in front with his hands on the ground, the mother with her arms around his waist, and the naked baby resting on the mother's shoulder. The facial features are quite realistically modeled. Both the baby and the father are wearing bracelets. The man has long, loose hair and is wearing a short, tassled loincloth. The woman is wearing a skirt and a sort of cap on her head. A tubular spout comes out from the man's back, which is evidence that it was used as a vessel.
State of Colima
Shaft Tomb Culture
Proto-Classic, 200 B.C.- A.D. 200
Ceramic
Height: 17.2 cm
Width: 18 cm

48. FAMILY

The family formed the basic unifying element of Mesoamerican society. In this family scene, besides highlighting daily life there is an allusion to the happiness of communal living and play, and to the identification of the children with their parents.
State of Colima
Shaft Tomb Culture
Proto-Classic, 200 B.C.- A.D. 200
Ceramic
Height: 7.7 cm
Width: 5.4 cm

49. YOUNG WOMAN

This delicately modeled clay sculpture is one of the most elegant ceramic testimonies from the center of Veracruz; in it we observe a young woman with a graceful silhouette, her breasts exposed. The perforations in the upper part of her head are a peculiar element, which indicate that the statue was originally decorated with feathers or flowers incrusted as her hair.
Provenience Unknown
Classical Central Veracruz Culture
Classic, A.D. 300-900
Ceramic
Height: 45.5 cm
Width: 32 cm

50. ADOLESCENT

In Pre-Hispanic imagery there was little inclination to represent frankly sexual themes. This sculpture of a nude adolescent with an erect penis is associated with the glorification of masculine fertility because of its phallic character.
Texcoco, State of Mexico
Aztec
Late Post-Classic, A.D. 1300-1521
Ceramic
Height: 55 cm
Width: 20 cm

51. MATERNITY
Among the Aztec, parents at the birth of a child would send for a priest in charge of fortelling destiny. The so-called "tonalpouhque," would read from a book containing the calendar of rituals and would thus be able to give the child the secret name that corresponded with his day of birth. In this figurine of a mother with her child, it is possible to observe the black lines which define the details of the piece.
Tlatelolco, City of Mexico
Aztec
Late Post-Classic, A.D. 1300-1521
Ceramic
Height: 16.8 cm
Width: 10.4 cm

52. MATERNITY
Women in Pre-Columbian societies were considered ready for marriage when they reached sexual maturity. From this moment on they would be valued for an abundant fertility which is why in these figurines the women are represented as always carrying a child in their arms.
Provenience Unknown
Toltec
Early Post-Classic, A.D. 900-1500
Ceramic
Height: 16 cm
Width: 8.5 cm

53. MATERNITY
Some of the various communities of Mesoamerica performed practices of personal embellishment such as cranial deformation at the time of birth. Newborns would have wood slats placed against their heads and held in place by textile or leather bandages in order to achieve this deformation. In this figurine from the Huastec region, we can see a mother suckling her child.
Panuco, Veracruz
Huastec
Classic, A.D. 300-900
Ceramic
Height: 30 cm
Width: 9.5 cm

54. MATERNITY
Daily life in indigenous societies demanded all the attention and efforts of the women. From the first hours of the morning they were occupied with the preparation of food, the making of clothes for the entire family, and with caring for their children. This is what we see in this figurine where the mother is lovingly hugging her child while taking food to the family.
State of Colima
Shaft Tomb Culture
Proto-Classic, 200 B.C.-A.D. 200
Ceramic
Height: 12 cm
Width: 5.5 cm

55. MATERNITY
From the time of birth until the age of 4 or 5, children learned how to walk, talk, and live with the other members of the family. In this first stage of infancy, mothers were responsible for transmitting to their children the principles of life in society, as can be gathered from this figurine in which a Teotihuacan woman carries her child straddled on her waist.
Teotihuacan
Teotihuacan, State of Mexico
Classic, 100 B.C.- A.D. 650
Ceramic
Height: 12 cm
Width: 7.3 cm

56. TEOTIHUACAN LADY
In these delicate representations modeled in clay, we can appreciate the women of Teotihuacan who with great elegance display the clothing that was the style of those times: long skirts and a type of blouse that covered the arms. The considerable size of the headdresses that were probably made from amate, (or Mexican fig tree), paper with stick or wood frames is admirable.
Teotihuacan
Teotihuacan, State of Mexico
Classic, 100 B.C.- A.D. 650
Ceramic
Height: 8.8 cm
Width: 6 cm

57. TEOTIHUACAN LADY
Because of the climactic conditions of the central valleys of Mexico, no examples of weavings made during the Pre-Hispanic era have been conserved. This is why it is important to study the clay figurines which show us the types of clothing: often through incisions or paint the ceramicists would suggest the lines and design of the textiles.
Teotihuacan, State of Mexico
Teotihuacan
Classic, 100 B.C.-A.D. 650
Ceramic
Height: 7.9 cm
Width: 5.5 cm

58. TEOTIHUACAN LADY
The Teotihuacan artisans with great ability created thousands of small clay figurines, hand-made or made from molds, that are a portrait of that society; this includes women, as can be appreciated in this piece. She displays circular earspools and necklaces of several strands.
Teotihuacan, State of Mexico
Teotihuacan
Classic, 100 B.C.-A.D. 650
Ceramic
Height: 4.4 cm
Width: 3 cm

59. THE WOMAN MILLER
One of the principal daily activities of indigenous women in the Pre-Hispanic era and today is the preparation of "tortillas," a staple of Mexico. This figurine depicts with great realism the way in which the stones, called "manos" and "metates," are used for grinding corn into pulp.
Aztec
Valley of Mexico
Late Post-Classic, A.D. 1300-1521
Ceramic
Height: 12.2 cm
Width: 5.7 cm

60. THE WEAVER
It is because of the presence of these realistic creations in modeled clay that we are able to study the activities of everyday life of the Maya people. Here we have a woman that is weaving with a backstrap loom. The ceramicist gave this composition a humorous touch by adding a bird resting on the trunk against which the loom is supported.
Jaina
Maya, State of Campeche
Classic, A.D. 300-900
Ceramic
Height: 8 cm
Width: 12 cm

61. MALE TORSO
The sculptors of ancient Tenochitlan inherited the ancestral tradition, begun in the times of the Olmecs, of work on hard rocks, a material with which they skillfully carved. This torso, for example, can be appreciated for its realistic—almost portrait-like—depiction of a man in the fullness of virility with the physical traits that characterized this ethnic group: the prominent cheekbones, wide nose, thick lips, straight, black hair, and the absence of facial or body hair.
Aztec
Valley of Mexico
Late Post-Classic, A.D. 1300-1521
Stone
Height: 33 cm
Width: 20 cm

62. WOMAN
Exclusive to the Shaft Tomb Culture was the tradition of excavating tombs of great depth that communicated with the surface through shafts similar to those of wells. In these subterranean chambers they would deposit the deceased along with figures such as this one. It represents an adult woman with the dominant standard of beauty of that era of physical strength portrayed as wide hips to facilitate childbirth.
Shaft Tomb Culture
State of Nayarit
Proto-Classic, 200 B.C.-A.D. 200
Ceramic
Height: 67.2 cm
Width: 29.7 cm

63. THE OLD SOWER
A constant in the iconography of Huastec art is the presence of old men with deformed skulls and shaved heads. They hold a staff or planting stick which indicated their intimate relation with the cult of masculine fertility and at the same time, with agriculture.
Provenience Unknown
Huastec
Post-Classic, A.D. 900-1521
Stone
Height: 57 cm
Width: 32 cm

64. AILING OLD WOMAN
According to the studies of physical anthropologists, average life expectancy among the indigenous societies of Pre-Hispanic Mexico is considered to have been between 35 and 40 years of age. Those individuals who were able to reach old age were thought to be repositories of tradition and knowledge. In this realistic figurine we have an old woman who places her hand to her mouth in a convulsive contraction of pain.
Jaina
Maya, State of Campeche
Classic, A.D. 300-900
Ceramic
Height: 15 cm
Width: 6 cm

65. OLD MAN
From the first works of art created by the Mesoamerican communities, the theme of human old age has been one of the most represented. In Teotihuacan culture these images of decrepit men received the greatest worship because of their association with the fire cult and the ancestral deities. This unique figure is an example of this ritual art, in which the artist created the artifice of giving movement to the head.
Teotihuacan, State of Mexico
Teotihuacan
Classic, A.D. 100-650
Ceramic
Height: 16 cm
Width: 10.4 cm

66. HEAD OF A DEAD MAN
The image of death is constantly present in Aztec art. Here they portrayed an individual at the moment of his death.
Provenience Unknown
Aztec
Late Post-Classic, A.D. 1300-1521
Stone
Height: 30 cm
Width: 22 cm

67. SKULL

Truly impressive is this large skull of modeled clay. The artist gave to the skull the vital quality of the relationship between life and death by modeling the orbs of the eyes in such a way as to indicate the presence of life in the skeleton. The piece presents two lateral holes that symbolize those necessary for the skull of the victim to hang on wooden poles in Aztec public skull rack, called "Tzompantli".
Valley of Mexico
Aztec
Late Post-Classic, A.D. 1300-1521
Ceramic
Height: 22 cm
Width: 27 cm

68. WOMAN WHO DIED IN CHILD BIRTH

Among the Aztec, women who died in childbirth were considered warriors who gave their life on the battlefield and thus, their image represented a clear allusion to death and the underworld, the kingdom of the dead. In this sculpture we can appreciate how the artist insists on this macabre iconography with the use of the diadem made of skulls and the necklace made of skulls and cut-off hands. The altar that supports the image is also decorated with human skulls in profile. The altar originates from an excavation in Mexico City.
Calixtlahuaca, State of Mexico
Aztec
Late Post-Classic, A.D. 1200-1521
Stone
Height: 1.1 meters
Width: 54.5 cm

69. GOD OF THE WIND

The wind was deified as "Ehecatl" through association with the ancestral god called, by Nahuatl speakers, "Quetzalcoatl." This god, Ehecatl-Quetzalcoatl, was imagined to have the body of a man with a half-mask of a bird's beak which permitted the god to form the wind. This sculpture, unique in its genre, presents Ehecatl as a fat person with a prominent skull resulting from artificial deformation. The deity holds two serpents that wrap themselves along his back.
Provenience Unknown
Aztec
Late Post-Classic, A.D. 1300-1521
Stone
Height: 60 cm
Width: 38 cm

70. TLACUACHE PRIEST

The Zapotecs of Monte Alban were great sculptors of fired clay. They modeled with great elegance the images of gods and priests such as this figure that represents an individual wearing as a helmet the head of a curious American mammal like an opossum. One can observe within the animal's head the delicate details of the priest's face. Among the elements of his costume is the remarkable large breastplate which rises above the shoulders and the belt of large shells that served as bells.
Monte Alban, State of Oaxaca
Zapotec
Classic, A.D. 300-900
Ceramic
Height: 66.5 cm
Width: 33 cm

71. TABLET OF THE PIERCED HEART

Constantly present in Toltec iconography are themes of war and sacrifice, as in this tablet, where two pairs of arrows pierce a bleeding heart surrounded by spirals and stylized flowers.
Tula, State of Hidalgo
Toltec
Early Post-Classic, A.D. 900-1300
Stone
Height: 59 cm
Width: 60 cm

72. TABLET OF APARICIO

In the ball game ritual, the culminating moment was dedicated to the decapitation of one of the players, which is the theme of this tablet. Along with four others, this one decorated the vertical walls of a playing field. The seated player has in place of his head seven snakes corresponding to the number of currents of blood that sprung up after his decapitation. Both the number seven and the serpent are related to the fertility of the earth.
Aparicio, State of Veracruz
Classic Central Veracruz Culture
Classic, A.D. 300-900
Stone
Height: 1.27 meters
Width: 54 cm

73. SOLAR GOD

The Maya ceramicists of Palenque worked molded clay with unequaled skill. They created true sculptures such as this elongated tube in which we can recognize the solar god Ah K'in, with his protruding nose and headdress in which a stylized animal stands out. It is possible to appreciate the dental mutilation characteristic of the deity.
Palenque, State of Chiapas
Maya
Classic, A.D. 300-900
Ceramic
Height: 95 cm
Width: 35 cm

74. DOG WITH MASK

These sculptures are very popular with students of Pre-Hispanic indigenous art. They are sculptures molded of finely polished red clay representing "itzcuintli," native hairless dogs, which were excessively fed and even used as food. This animal served as a guide for the dead in their travels through the underworld. This unusual piece shows us a canine wearing a human mask, a direct allusion to its participation in mortuary rites.

State of Colima
Shaft Tomb Culture
Proto-Classic, 200 B.C.-A.D. 200
Ceramic
Height: 20 cm
Width: 12 cm

75. OLMEC MAN

Stylization is the characteristic of this small sculpture carved from jade in the Olmec tradition. In this piece we can observe that the artist's purpose is to elongate in an exaggerated way the stature of the person that shows the typical Olmec face with traits of a jaguar.

Provenience Unknown
Olmec
Middle Pre-Classic, 1200-600 B.C.
Stone
Height: 14.5 cm
Width: 7 cm

76. LIFE AND DEATH

All of the Mexican Pre-Hispanic communities had among their most important religious principles the concept of duality. In this sculptural clay fragment we can observe the head of a person divided in half, one part being skeletal and the other covered with flesh, a clear allusion to the confrontation of life and death.

Zoyaltepec, State of Oaxaca
Zapotec
Classic, A.D. 600-900
Ceramic
Height: 37.7 cm
Width: 32.8 cm

77. HEAD OF XIPE TOTEC

For many of the peoples of ancient Mexico, the deity that was patron of both the change in vegetation—with the arrival of rains—and the art of gold and silver work was called Xipe Totec. He was represented as a man dressed in the skin of a victim flayed during sacrifice. This head is part of a larger sculpture and on it can be seen the skin that was used as a mask.

Mexico City
Aztec
Late Post-Classic, A.D. 1300-1521
Ceramic
Height: 30 cm
Width: 17 cm

78. HUNCHBACKED OLD MAN

Truly attractive is this figure modeled in clay, an image of an old man with many wrinkles on his face. He leans on a staff and stands on a mythological animal which takes the form a two-headed fish. It is believed that the man is the supernatural protector of fish.

State of Colima
Shaft Tomb Culture
Proto-Classic, 200 B.C.-A.D. 200
Ceramic
Height: 41.5 cm
Width: 24 cm

79. HUNCHBACKED MAN

The realism of this figure shows us a deformed being who has two humps: his rib cage and his back. The Aztecs believed that hunchbacks, albinos, Siamese twins, and especially dwarves were the children of the sun. For this reason the king Moctezuma had them confined to a special house in Tenochtitlan.

Valley of Mexico
Aztec
Late Post-Classic, A.D. 1300-1521
Stone
Height: 33 cm
Width: 17 cm

80. HUNCHBACKED MAN

The ceramicists of the Colima region developed great skill. With their hands they would recreate the daily and ceremonial life of their villages. Some deformed or sick persons were depicted with great realism given that these figures functioned as companions for the dead in the mortuary rites of the Shaft Tomb culture.

State of Colima
Shaft Tomb Culture
Proto-Classic, 200 B.C.-A.D. 200
Ceramic
Height: 32.4 cm
Width: 18 cm

81. SICK WOMAN

The realism with which this figure is treated is notable given that it shows us a naked woman revealing the symptoms of her illness: rashes or pustules that cover her entire body, but especially the breasts and stomach. On her face is reflected the pain and weeping caused by this illness, which in ancient times was considered a punishment by the gods.

State of Nayarit
Shaft Tomb Culture
Proto-Classic, 200 B.C.-A.D. 200
Ceramic
Height: 18.2 cm
Width: 13.2 cm

82. MASK

Abstraction and geometrization are the canons that determine the style of the Mezcala river region. The stone workers chose to work in semi-precious stones such as (in this case) obsidian, which is a volcanic crystal. Here it is used to carve these enigmatic faces with protruding noses.

Templo Mayor, City of Mexico
Aztec-Mezcala
Late Post-Classic, A.D. 1300-1521
Obsidian
Height: 11.1 cm
Width: 10 cm

83. MASK

During the Pre-Classic or village era, in the ceremonies or celebrations, people used masks of fired clay such as this one that represents a grotesque person. This mask has perforations in the eyes, nose, and the upper corners which could have been used in a humorous scenic representation.
Tlatilco, State of Mexico
Pre-Classic High Central Plateau
Pre-Classic, 1200-100 B.C.
Ceramic
Height: 17.7 cm
Width: 16.4 cm

84. MASK

During the Aztec dominion over diverse regions of the High Central Plateau, funereal and ceremonial masks adopted a more realistic aspect. In this beautiful alabaster carving we can observe in the hollows of the eyes the traces of drills used in its fabrication.
Aztec
State of Puebla
Late Post-Classic, 1325-1521 A.D.
Alabaster
Height: 22 cm
Width: 23 cm

85. MASK

During the excavations of the Templo Mayor of México-Tenochtitlan, numerous masks originating from the state of Guerrero were discovered. They were deposited as offerings for the principal deities of the Aztec. These pieces have been considered to be among the precious objects that the Aztec demanded as tribute. Within the collection of Mezcala-style masks there are some that are characterized for the type of stylized "t" that is formed by the crossing of the nose-line and eye brows.
Templo Mayor, Mexico City
Aztec-Mezcala
Late Post-Classic, A.D. 1300-1521
Stone
Height: 15.9 cm
Width: 14.4 cm

86. MASK

The large format censers or incense burners made in Teotihuacan had as their central element the face of a deity that was modeled according to the canons of Teotihuacan masks. Like an inverted triangle, the mask was that of an unfeeling young adult.
Teotihuacan, State of Mexico
Teotihuacan
Classic, 100 B.C.-A.D. 650
Ceramic
Height: 9.5 cm
Width: 11.5 cm

87. SCENOGRAPHIC URN

During the archaeological excavations at Teotihuacan, numerous clay urns were discovered in the sacred precincts. This is an example of these miniature altars. Its decorative motifs consist of stylized birds, feathers, and other designs that are in reality small molded platelets adhering to the larger figure.
Teotihuacan, State of Mexico
Teotihuacan
Classic, 100 B.C.-A.D. 650
Ceramic
Height: 46 cm
Width: 40 cm

88. THE DANCER

The village societies from the formative era have left us a more intimate testimonial of their daily life. This includes innumerable modeled clay figurines of shamans, acrobats, or dancers that combine both ritual and game in their representation. In this small figure the intention of expressing the dancer's movement by tilting the head to one side enhances the charm of the piece.
Tlatilco, State of Mexico
Pre-Classic High Central Plateau
Pre-Classic, 1200-100 B.C.
Ceramic
Height: 7 cm
Width: 5 cm

89. THE MUSICIAN

Many of the figurines originating from West Mexico are representations of musicians which serve as material proof of the numerous ceremonies and festivities with which the community celebrated the different annual events, especially those relating to agriculture and military conquests. This figure is playing a percussion instrument while simultaneously singing.
State of Nayarit
Shaft Tomb Culture
Proto-Classic, 200 B.C.-A.D. 200
Ceramic
Height: 18.4 cm
Width: 10.9 cm

90. THE MUSICIAN

Of the instruments used by the ancient Mexicans the two most common were the wind instruments, such as flutes or whistles, and the percussion instruments such as drums of large proportions as depicted in this figure. The Nayarit tradition of using numerous ear and nose rings can also be distinguished in this piece.
State of Nayarit
Shaft Tomb Culture
Proto-Classic, 200 B.C.-A.D. 200
Ceramic
Height: 13 cm
Width: 7.5 cm

91. THE MUSICIAN

In the central valleys of Mexico one of the most typical musical instruments is called "Huehuetl" or "Tlapanhuehuetl" that was made from a hollowed out tree trunk later covered with an animal skin. Sound was produced by banging rubber-coated wooden strikers. This instrument can be seen in this figurine.
Tlatelolco, City of Mexico
Aztec
Late Post-Classic, A.D. 1300-1521
Ceramic
Height: 9.7 cm
Width: 3.4 cm

92. THE EAGLE-WARRIOR MUSICIAN

In the great ceremonies of México-Tenochtitlan warriors participated by singing and dancing, as is observed in this small figurine of an eagle-warrior who wears his military apparel and plays the "tlapanhuehuetl".
Tlatelolco, Mexico City
Aztec
Late Post-Classic, A.D. 1300-1521
Ceramic
Height: 15.6 cm
Width: 6.8 cm